Regional Perspectives on World Development Report 1995

W0037738

LABOR AND THE GROWTH CRISIS IN SUB-SAHARAN AFRICA

THE WORLD BANK

WASHINGTON, D.C.

© 1995 The International Bank for Reconstruction and Development / The World Bank
1818 H Street, N.W., Washington, D.C. 20433, U.S.A.

First printing August 1995

This report has been prepared by the staff of the World Bank. The judgments expressed do not necessarily reflect the views of the Board of Executive Directors or the governments they represent.

Editing, layout, and production by American Writing Corporation

ISBN 0-8213-3343-7
ISSN 1020-3648

Contents

This report was prepared in conjunction with *World Development Report 1995: Workers in an Integrating World*. It was written by David L. Lindauer under the direction of Michael Walton. He was assisted by Deon Filmer. Alison Strong edited the report. Christian Perez laid out the text. Several people provided useful comments, including Arvil Van Adams, Paul Collier, Shanta Devarajan, Ian Heggie, William Steel, Elisabeth Stock, and Ann Velenchik.

Foreword

Over the past three decades workers in Sub-Saharan Africa have experienced little improvement in their economic circumstances. Nearly two of every three workers continue to be engaged in agricultural activities and receive little for their efforts. In 1993 output per worker was only marginally greater than it had been in 1965, and without sustained increases in labor productivity it is impossible for wages to rise.

There are many reasons for the disappointing economic performance of the region. Civil wars and social unrest have wreaked havoc in many countries. External shocks were a contributing factor. But much of the explanation lies with the choice of economic policies. Labor's interests were poorly served by strategies that relied more on government control of the economy than on market forces and that were inward looking and biased against the rural economy. When economies in Sub-Saharan Africa crashed in the 1980s, even those workers privileged by the prevailing system could no longer be protected from market forces, and they, along with the others, bore the costs of adjustment.

These experiences have resulted in a "silent revolution" in economic thinking. In many countries overvalued exchange rates have been reduced dramatically. Price controls and other forms of direct intervention are being removed. But much remains to be done. Sub-Saharan Africa is still marginalized in the world economy. The region's exports, the foreign investments it attracts, and the migrants it sends abroad do not represent significant shares of world totals. African workers have much to gain from the global economy. But for them to achieve those gains, further macroeconomic and institutional reform is required, including a significant reduction in the risks of investing in the region.

Labor market reform belongs on the region's agenda. Most workers in Sub-Saharan Africa are beyond the reach of direct government interventions in the labor market yet have been hurt by past attempts to increase wages or expand employment by government fiat. Labor policies need to be attuned to market realities. That is no less true for public employment, which has been a drag on economic growth. Improved public sector performance requires pay and employment reforms, but also institutional reforms and a rethinking of the feasible scope of government activity.

What are the prospects for workers in Sub-Saharan Africa as they enter the next century? There is a risk that the world economy will move on, leaving much of Africa behind. But that need not be the case. The right combination of domestic and international policies could generate employment, increase productivity, and raise wages for Sub-Saharan Africa's expanding labor force.

Edward V. K. Jaycox
Vice President
Africa Region

Summary

World Development Report 1995: Workers in an Integrating World looks at what is required to improve labor outcomes in low- and middle-income economies. The Report identifies four areas in need of policy reform: development strategy, international integration, labor market interventions, and transformation to greater market orientation.

This report considers the relevance of these policy areas to Sub-Saharan African circumstances. Three key messages emerge:

■ A market-based approach to development, by expanding markets and encouraging more productive investments, will be a labor-demanding strategy in Africa as it has been elsewhere and is key to improving labor outcomes.

■ Sub-Saharan Africa has become increasingly marginalized in the world economy. It is in the interest of Africa's labor force that this trend be reversed and that the region increase its integration with and participation in global markets.

■ Domestic labor market policies, especially those governing workers in the public sector, need to be redesigned to encourage more efficient use of labor and nonlabor resources. Required are policies that better reflect the labor market conditions in individual economies.

This report begins with a review of labor market outcomes in Sub-Saharan Africa. It then analyzes what is required to realize more rapid economic growth through the increased accumulation and productivity of physical and human capital. It examines Africa's role in the world economy and why greater integration is essential to the region. It discusses the role of labor policies directed at both private and public employers and considers how Sub-Saharan African workers are affected by the transition from closed to more open development strategies. It concludes with a brief review of the prospects for Africa's growing labor force.

CHAPTER 1

A Profile of Workers

There are an estimated 314 million men and women of working age (fifteen to sixty-four years old) in Sub-Saharan Africa—9 percent of the world's working-age population. Most earn little for their efforts, which is why 40 percent of the population in Sub-Saharan Africa continues to live in poverty.[1]

Most Africans of working age are working (Figure 1a). Slightly more than six of ten workers are engaged in agriculture, most in smallholder farming (Figure 1b). About one in ten is employed in industry (manufacturing, mining, construction, and utilities), and the rest are in services (commerce, trade, government, and personal services). Most African workers work on their own farms or in informal household enterprises. Wage employment in industry and services occupies only an estimated 12 percent of the labor force, a somewhat smaller percentage than that in low-income economies in South and East Asia. Twenty-one percent of Sub-Saharan Africa's labor force is engaged in the informal sector, defined here as self-employment or unpaid work in nonagricultural family enterprises.[2]

About a third of the working-age population is considered not employed, most because they are raising children or caring for their families, some because they are attending school, and others because they are unable to work or to find employment. Of the 100 million working-age Africans not counted as part of the labor force, 80 percent are women. A similar proportion holds in East Asia and Latin America.[3] What these numbers reflect is women's greater involvement in work in the household and the somewhat arbitrary definition of labor force participation.

Official unemployment, defined as those seeking work but unable to find any, is estimated at 6 percent of the labor force. Estimates vary considerably across countries, and the difficulty of defining and measuring unemployment in agrarian economies makes these estimates poor indicators of the underutilization of labor in the region (Box 1).

In addition to the labor force between the ages of fifteen and sixty-four, the International Labour Organization (ILO) estimates that there are 7 million workers aged sixty-five and over, and some 16 million children between the ages of ten and fourteen, working in Sub-Saharan Africa. But the number of child workers is underestimated in all economies, more so where agriculture predominates, so the actual number of child workers in Sub-Saharan Africa is likely to be many millions more.

Most working-age Africans are working, and more than half are working in agriculture

Figure 1a. Distribution of the working-age population in Sub-Saharan Africa

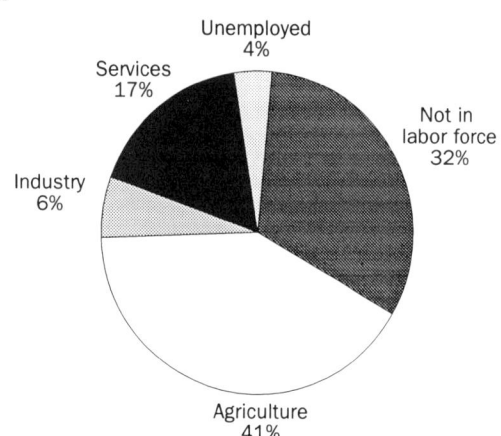

Figure 1b. Distribution of the labor force in Sub-Saharan Africa

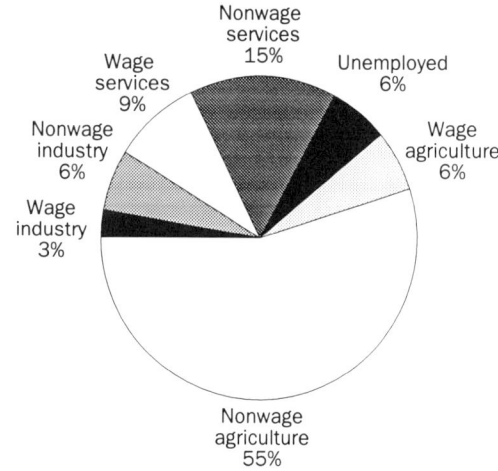

Note: Data for Figure 1a are projected from a sample of 314 million people in countries of the region. Data for Figure 1b are projected from a sample of 214 million people aged fifteen to sixty-four in countries of the region.
Source: ILO 1986 and ILO data updates; ILO, *Yearbook of Labor Statistics,* various years; country sources.

Box 1. How much unemployment is there in Sub-Saharan Africa?

Most quoted unemployment rates are based on the International Labor Organization definition: people above a specified age who, during the reference period (for example, the past week), are without work, currently available for work, and seeking work. By this definition, the unemployed usually account for a small percentage of the working-age population, especially in countries with a large rural population where working on the family farm or working for others on a casual basis is common. But behind the single figure for unemployment lies a deeper story of underutilized labor.

Box Table 1 reports measures of the incidence of unemployment and underemployment in Ghana and South Africa, two countries for which appropriate surveys are available. In Ghana, where almost 60 percent of the labor force is engaged in agriculture, open unemployment is very low. But almost a quarter of the labor force worked no more than fifteen hours in the week before the survey, not necessarily by choice but because work is unavailable and highly seasonal. In South Africa the picture is different. Agriculture occupies only 7 percent of the labor force, and open unemployment is high. But even higher is the share of working-age people who report themselves as discouraged—that is, those who have given up looking for work because they believe none is available. Because of the number of discouraged workers, the share of South Africa's black working-age population classified as out of the labor force is high. Taken together, the indicators of unemployment and underemployment in South Africa suggest a staggeringly high measure of lost productive potential.

Who are the unemployed? Again, comparing Ghana and South Africa gives two different pictures. In Ghana some 80 percent of those unemployed or discouraged are in urban areas, and 60 percent of those working zero to fifteen hours a week are in rural areas. The young are disproportionately represented among the unemployed: those aged twenty to twenty-four are 15 percent of the working-age population, but 30 percent of unemployed and discouraged workers. Women are overrepresented among those out of the labor force and constitute more than 60 percent of those working few hours—excluding hours worked in the home. In Ghana unemployment rates tend to increase with schooling level attained. In urban areas those with no schooling are almost 40 percent of the working-age population, but only 20 percent of unemployed and discouraged workers. Unemployed and discouraged workers tend not to be among the lowest income groups. Relative poverty, especially in rural areas, is most often associated with working few hours.

In South Africa's black population unemployment is higher among the young but not overwhelmingly so: those aged twenty to twenty-four are almost 20 percent of the working-age population and about 25 percent of the unemployed and discouraged. Unemployed and discouraged workers and those who work few hours have about the same education as the rest of the working-age population. Unlike in Ghana, relative poverty in South Africa is greatest among those who are unemployed or discouraged, especially in rural areas.

Two different employment pictures emerge

Box Table 1. Employment indicators for Ghana and South Africa
(percentage of category)

Category	Out of the labor force	Discouraged	Unemployed	Working 0 to 15 hours
Ghana (1988–89)				
Labor force	—	—	1.6	24.5
Labor force and discouraged workers	—	1.5	1.6	24.1
Working-age population	24.1	1.1	1.2	18.3
South Africa[a] (1993)				
Labor force	—	—	16.0	7.4
Labor force and discouraged workers	—	25.5	11.9	5.5
Working-age population	38.1	15.8	7.4	3.4

— Not applicable.
a. Black population only.
Source: Ghana Living Standards Survey, 1988–89 data; South African Project for Statistics on Living Standards and Development, 1993 data.

Returns to work activity—earnings or the value of own production, or both—are low throughout Sub-Saharan Africa. Although data on earnings are not widely available for the region, the results of a recent international survey suggest how modern sector wages in Sub-Saharan Africa compare with those in other regions. In purchasing power parity (PPP) terms, workers in Nairobi, Kenya, almost regardless of occu-pation, earn less than their counterparts in India and often dramatically less than workers in many middle- and high-income economies (Table 1). And since urban workers earn far more than those engaged in agriculture—the majority of African workers—most Africans earn very little both absolutely and relative to workers in much of the rest of the world.

Workers in Nairobi earn less — often dramatically less — than their counterparts in other regions

Table 1. The international wage hierarchy, 1994

City	GNP per capita (1993 U.S. dollars)	Ratio of GNP per capita (PPP) to Kenya's	Ratio of annual earnings to those of female industrial workers in Nairobi, Kenya				
			Engineer	Skilled industrial worker	Bus driver	Construction worker	Female industrial worker
Frankfurt	23,560	13.1	56	31	27	20	18
Seoul	7,660	7.5	26	16	16	12	10
Bogota	1,400	4.3	38	11	8	3	10
Budapest	3,350	4.7	10	6	7	5	4
Jakarta	740	2.4	13	9	4	4	1
Bombay	300	0.9	7	5	6	3	4
Nairobi	270	1.0	8	3	1	<1	1

Note: GNP per capita figures refer to the nation in which each city is located. Earnings ratios are based on earnings adjusted for purchasing power parity (PPP).
Source: Union Bank of Switzerland 1994; World Bank 1995c.

CHAPTER 2

Improved Labor Outcomes the Exception

For most of the past decade improvements in labor outcomes in Sub-Saharan Africa have been the exception rather than the rule. This is evident from trends in GDP per worker (Box 2). For the region as a whole GDP per worker grew by only 1.2 percent a year between 1965 and 1980, but between 1980 and 1993 the growth in GDP per worker turned negative, averaging –1.0 percent a year.

The regional average, constructed by weighting countries by the size of their working-age population, is dominated by Sub-Saharan Africa's most populous nations: Ethiopia, Nigeria, South Africa, and Zaire (these four together account for nearly half the region's working-age population). Although the weak performance of these four economies accounts for much of the aggregate trend in GDP per worker, much of the rest of Africa has followed a similar path (Figure 2). Estimates of labor productivity by country show some variance—including strong performance by Botswana, Lesotho, Mauritius, and Seychelles. But the conclusion remains that for most Sub-Saharan African countries, and 75 percent of the region's work force, labor productivity today is lower than in 1980, and for many

nations, suffering the effects of a long economic decline, it is lower than in 1965.

Pay and employment outcomes show many signs of the economic stagnation and decline in the region. Workers in the formal economy have experienced large declines in the real value of their wages (Figure 3). In Ghana in 1984, real earnings in wage employment in agriculture, manufacturing, and the public sector had plummeted to between 15 and 25 percent of their value a decade earlier. If household incomes had fallen by as much, many families would have starved. Instead, households adjusted—some urban workers took multiple jobs, others migrated back to rural areas—but many experienced significant erosion in their standard of living.

Not only did real wages collapse, but the formal sector's share of employment grew very little. Between the 1960s and the late 1980s the working-age population more than doubled in Côte d'Ivoire, Ghana, and Tanzania. In Ghana and Tanzania the overall structure of employment stayed relatively constant, with little change in the shares of the work force in agriculture and in self-employment and wage employment

---

Box 2. Labor productivity as a measure of labor outcomes

We focus on GDP per worker, an approximation of average labor productivity in an economy, for two reasons. First, more direct measures of labor outcomes—such as trends in real wages, in growth in employment opportunities, or in unemployment—are generally unavailable. In addition, in agrarian economies measures of labor market outcomes designed for formal urban employment are inappropriate. And labor market information in Sub-Saharan Africa is scarce.*

Second, improvements in labor outcomes depend on improvements in labor productivity. With growth in output per worker, workers can receive more for their efforts. For farm households (or household enterprises) that employ only family members, the association between rising labor productivity and increasing returns to work activity is straightforward—if each family worker produces more, the family will consume more. The same relationship holds in

more formal and impersonal employment relationships. With growing labor productivity, employers not only are able to pay more, they also are compelled to do so, because they must compete with other employers for labor that is increasingly productive in different activities.

---

* An on-line ILO data compilation includes only thirteen African countries that since 1980 have undertaken a census or labor force survey and reported the results. After 1985 the number drops to four. For average earnings in manufacturing, data compiled by UNIDO provide valuable information; however, using only end-points, a growth rate can be calculated for only seven Sub-Saharan countries for 1970–90. Wage data on sectors other than manufacturing are harder to come by. National statistical publications must be relied on, but these are scarce, particularly after the mid-1980s.

For most Sub-Saharan African countries labor productivity today is lower than in 1980—and for many it is lower than in 1965

Figure 2. Rate of growth in GDP per worker, 1965–80 and 1980–93
(percent)

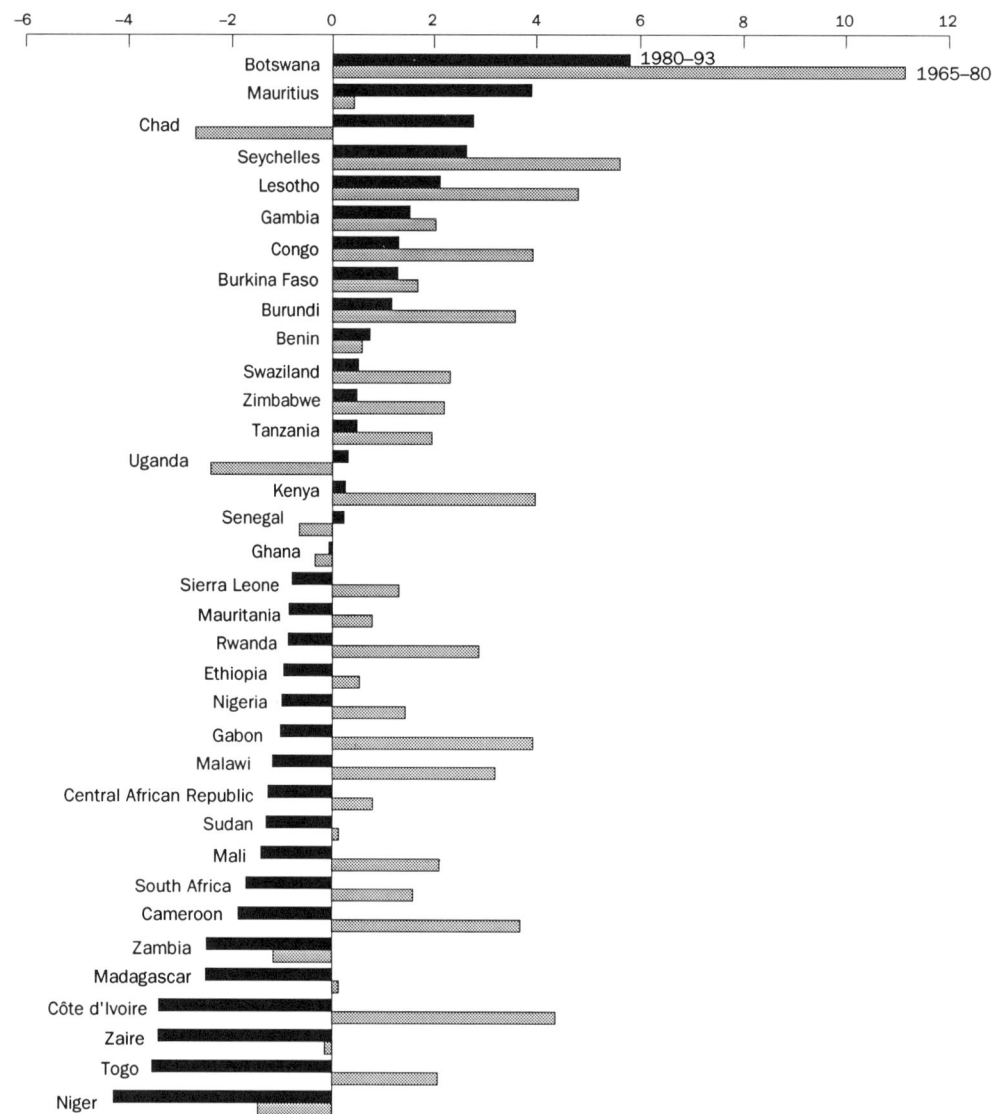

Source: World Bank data; ILO 1986 and ILO data updates.

outside agriculture (Table 2). In Côte d'Ivoire, which first went through a period of rapid growth followed by a sharp decline, labor force participation rates fell, especially among women, as the economy became more urban; correspondingly, the share of the labor force in agriculture declined and that in wage employment rose.

Over the past three decades South Africa's working-age population also has grown rapidly, nearly tripling since 1960. But the structure of employment is fundamentally different from that elsewhere in Sub-Saharan Africa. The increase in per capita income and in industrialization has created wage employment for 40 percent of the working-age population. But at the same time policies that included appropriating land from the black majority and squeezing the profitability of peasant farming have resulted in a dualistic economy that is perhaps without parallel—one in which a minuscule share of labor is in agriculture, the unemployment rate has more than doubled, and an extraordinary number of people are classified as out of the labor force.

Data for the rest of Sub-Saharan Africa suggest that agriculture continues to absorb and support a majority of workers. The number of unemployed and informal sector workers (proxied here by self-employed workers and unpaid family workers outside agriculture) has grown along with the labor force, but these economies have experienced little relative increase in either the open unemployment rate or informalization. But a narrower focus, on unemployment in major cities, suggests a different conclusion. Several studies report urban unemployment rates in Sub-Saharan Africa of 10 to 20 percent during the 1980s—rates that are thought to have increased over time.[4] But because urban areas still account for only a small percentage of the labor force—only 11 percent of the region's population resides in urban agglomerations of one million or more people—national unemployment rates remain low, and they have changed little over time.

• • •

Without more and better data, it is difficult to say precisely what the trends have been in individual countries in wages, open unemployment, the informalization of economies, or the incidence of poverty. But what can be said with certainty is that few nations in Sub-Saharan Africa have managed to avoid the past decade's downward trends in employment opportunities, returns to work activity, and labor productivity.

Formal sector workers have seen large declines in the real value of their wages

Figure 3. Trends in average real earnings in Ghana, Kenya, and Malawi, 1969–91
(1969=100)

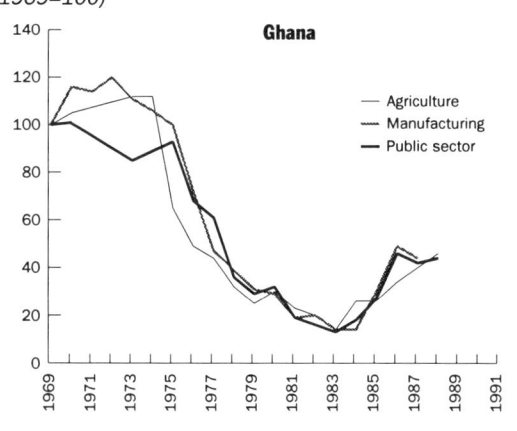

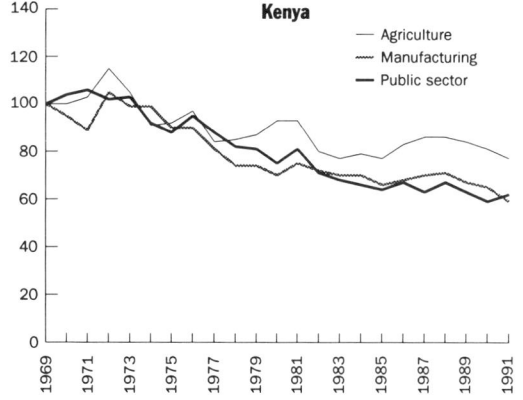

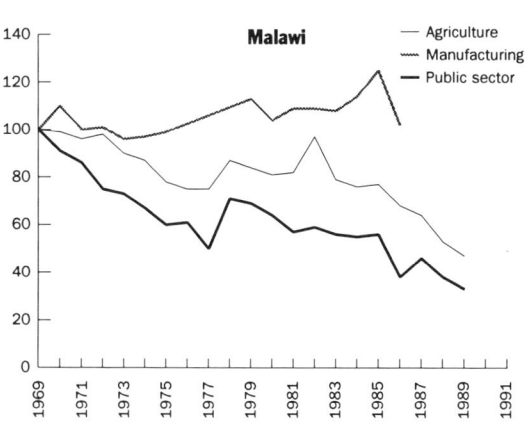

Source: UNIDO data; country sources.

Employment structures have remained fairly constant, especially where economic growth has stagnated

Table 2. Employment structure in selected countries, 1960s and 1980s

Category	Côte d'Ivoire		Ghana		South Africa		Tanzania	
	1964	1987	1960	1989	1960	1993	1967	1988
	Number of workers (thousands)							
Agricultural workers	1,743	2,611	1,559	3,426	1,523	950	4,856	10,118
Nonagricultural wage employees	131	536	385	928	3,005	8,864	424	1,162
Nonagricultural self-employed workers	143	429	585	1,372	417	890	143	650
Unemployed workers	84	107	152	171	301	1,508	106	111
Out of the labor force	259	1,294	832	1,883	3,354	10,095	547	1,047
Total (working-age population)[a]	2,360	4,870	3,513	7,780	8,600	22,304	6,076	13,088
	Share of total (percent)							
Agricultural workers	74	52	44	44	18	4	80	77
Nonagricultural wage employees	6	11	11	12	35	40	7	9
Nonagricultural self-employed workers	6	9	17	18	5	4	2	5
Unemployed workers	3	2	4	2	3	7	2	1
Out of the labor force	11	26	24	24	39	45	9	8
Total (working-age population)[a]	100	100	100	100	100	100	100	100

a. Working age is fifteen to sixty-four except for South Africa, for which it is defined here as twenty and over.
Source: ILO 1986 and updates; ILO, *Yearbook of Labor Statistics,* various years; Côte d'Ivoire Living Standards Survey, 1987 data; Ghana Living Standards Survey, 1988–89 data; South African Bureau of Statistics 1968; South African Project for Statistics on Living Standards and Development, 1994 data; Tanzania Bureau of Statistics 1971 and 1992.

CHAPTER 3

Problems of Labor Demand, Not Supply

Economic growth is good for workers. In East and South Asia accelerated growth in the 1980s benefited workers in two ways: the labor market spread wage increases to all sectors, and growth was associated with more workers securing employment in higher-productivity activities.

In Sub-Saharan Africa worsening labor outcomes are the result of decades of poor growth performance. The slow and often negative growth rates in the region can be traced to many factors, but among the most important have been policy failures. Labor's interests were not well served by inward-looking strategies that relied on overvalued currencies, restrictive trade policies, public enterprises, and a host of regulatory devices designed to protect the domestic economy and thwart market mechanisms.

Such strategies, at least initially, did produce benefits for a small number of "insiders"—mostly workers in the civil service, state enterprises, and foreign enclaves. But they left the majority of African workers—those in agriculture and the informal sector—with low returns on their labor. When the underlying strategy proved unviable and macroeconomic forces led to economic collapse, even "insiders" saw their earnings plummet. Today the need for new approaches is recognized across the region, although the pace of reform varies widely.

Determinants of growth

Economic growth depends on raising the productivity of all factors of production, including labor. That requires accumulation—investments by households and employers in physical capital, new technologies, and worker skills. Guided by market opportunities, accumulation raises labor productivity and makes possible long-run, economywide growth in household incomes.

But accumulation alone does not guarantee growth. In the wrong environment accumulation can result in unproductive or idle resources. The complex relationship between accumulation and economic growth is captured by cross-country data comparing long-run growth rates (1960–85) in GDP per worker with new estimates of the accumulation of physical capital and of the years of schooling of the work force.[5] In a sample of more than sixty low- and middle-income countries there is a positive correlation between accumulation and the growth in GDP per worker, although the correlation is far from perfect (Figure 4).

The data on growth and accumulation in Sub-Saharan Africa show why labor productivity has grown slowly. Two tendencies are apparent. First, Sub-Saharan Africa has accumulated less than other regions. Second, the physical and human capital that has been accumulated has often been less productive than capital in other regions. This is apparent in Figure 5, which shows that, for a given level of accumulation, Sub-Saharan African countries realized slower rates of productivity growth. The record on accumulation and growth in Sub-Saharan Africa suggests an environment that failed to encourage investment and, by misallocating resources, reduced their productivity.[6]

Several factors have reduced the effect of human capital investments in increasing labor productivity.[7] First, as is true for accumulating physical capital, increasing the education of the labor force is not enough to overcome an environment inimical to economic growth. Second, government policy has not always encouraged the best use of expenditures on education. Often the mix of inputs has been inappropriate (too much spending on school infrastructure and too little on supplies and teacher salaries), the quality of inputs has been low (poorly trained teachers), the standards required of graduates have been minimal, or the distribution of resources has been both inefficient and inequitable (promoting higher education for a select few at the expense of primary and secondary schooling).

To realize more rapid growth in their economies and in labor productivity, African countries must confront the dual problem of accumulating more capital, physical and human, and of more effectively utilizing the capital they already have.

Evidence from elsewhere

Evidence from other regions, especially East Asia, provides insight into what is needed to set in motion productive investment in physical and human capital. Many different factors helped set East Asia on a successful growth path, and countries in the region did not always pursue the same policies. But in all these economies labor was well served by macroeconomic stability and market-based development strategies. Included in these strategies was support for agriculture—initially the major labor-intensive sector—through relatively light taxation, investment in rural infrastructure, and, in some cases, land reform in support

Investment in physical and human capital is necessary for productivity growth but does not guarantee it

Figure 4. Physical and human capital accumulation and growth rate of GDP per worker in Sub-Saharan African and other developing countries, 1960–85
(percent)

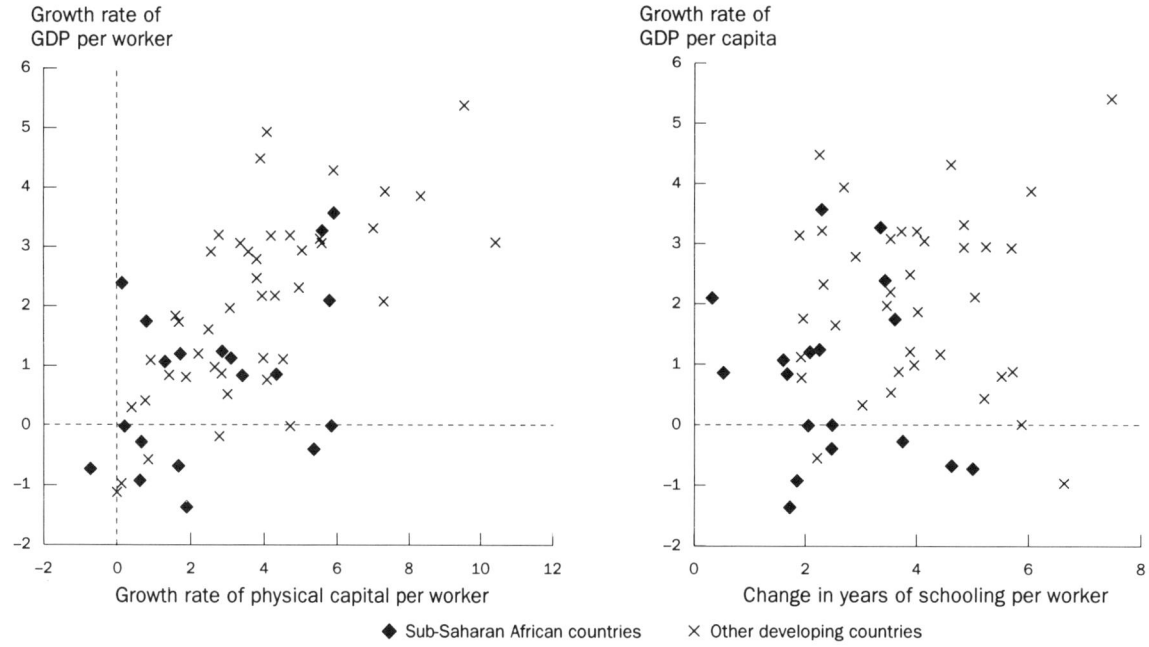

Note: Excludes high-income countries. Because these data refer to 1960–85, they capture little of the period (1980–93) of rapid decline in labor productivity in Sub-Saharan Africa and the Middle East and North Africa.
Source: Nehru and Dhareshwar 1991; Nehru, Swanson, and Dubey 1993.

of smallholder agriculture. By following comparative advantage and pursuing export markets, whether in primary products or manufactures, East Asian countries expanded their markets beyond their domestic economies and increased the demand for their labor.

At the same time, labor productivity increased as a result of high rates of investment in plant and equipment, acquisition of new technologies, and growth in the human capital of an expanding labor force, achieved through rapid increases in school enrollments and intensive firm-level training. These investments were financed through a combination of rising domestic savings rates and international capital, including loans and foreign direct investment.

Governments in East Asia intervened to varying degrees in their economies, but markets played an important role in directing the allocation of resources. The lesson of the importance of relying on the market can be drawn not only from the "economic miracle" of East Asia but also increasingly from the economic successes of reforming countries in Latin America (Chile and Peru), Eastern Europe (Estonia and Poland), and Sub-Saharan Africa (Ghana and Uganda) (Box 3).

Population growth, labor supply, and economic growth

Other regions not only show that market-based strategies are good for growth, they also demonstrate that population growth is not a persuasive explanation for the poor labor outcomes in Sub-Saharan Africa. In 1965–93 rates of growth of the working-age population were remarkably similar across regions. But growth in GDP varied enormously (Figure 5). Differences in the growth in output per worker must therefore be explained primarily by differences in the growth of labor demand.

Economic growth raises household incomes, which leads parents to choose to have fewer children and to provide them with more education. In time these household responses result in a labor force that grows more slowly and is more skilled. But when economies are stagnant and populations continue to grow rapidly, as in Sub-Saharan Africa, the dilemma of growth in the population, and thus in the future labor supply, remains. It takes about twenty years for lower fertility rates to show up in appreciably slower growth in a nation's labor supply. If the goal is to raise labor incomes, investments will bring a higher return if they encourage growth in labor demand. That will improve labor outcomes far sooner than will direct attempts to reduce the future labor supply.

Growth in the working-age population has been similar across regions, but GDP growth has not

Figure 5. Growth rates of working-age population and GDP in developing regions, 1965–93
(percent)

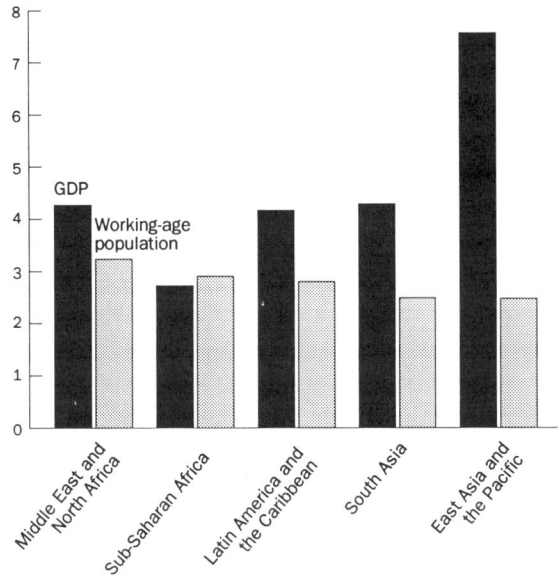

Source: World Bank data; ILO 1986 and ILO data updates.

Although slowing population growth is no substitute for efforts to increase labor demand, there is reason to emphasize social policies that contribute to fertility decline (educating girls, improving women's status, investing in reproductive health and family planning). These interventions can be justified on other grounds, specifically in terms of overcoming market failures (information failure concerning contraception, gender discrimination in education) and thereby contributing to the health and welfare of individuals and families.

The capabilities of workers

Improving labor outcomes requires an increase in labor demand. But labor supply also matters, especially the skills and capabilities of workers. The accumulation of human capital—through improvements in health and nutrition and the acquisition of schooling and training—can increase individual productivity and raise the economic return to work activity.

The importance of human capital has been recognized throughout Sub-Saharan Africa. In the past three decades the region has witnessed a huge expansion in schooling. Between 1965 and 1992 gross primary enrollment rates increased by more than half, from 41 percent to 67 percent, and gross secondary

enrollment rates more than quadrupled, from 4 percent to 18 percent.[8] That has meant a significant increase in the human capital of workers. Estimates suggest that mean years of schooling for the region's working-age population have risen from less than one in 1960 to more than three and a half years by 1995.[9] Yet the educational attainment of the labor force as a whole remains low because of the historic lack of schooling opportunities in the region. In addition, the increase in education has not been sustained. Gross enrollment rates for the region were higher in 1980 than they are today. This reversal, an effect of the region's economic stagnation, jeopardizes future growth.

Both the trend and the level of schooling in Sub-Saharan Africa raise two important questions. First, given increased enrollment, why have workers realized so little improvement in wages and employment opportunities? Second, is the low educational attainment itself a barrier to more rapid growth?

Part of the answer to the first question is that the accumulation of human capital is necessary but not sufficient for improving labor outcomes. This has been demonstrated in such countries as Cuba, Egypt, and Sri Lanka as well as in Sub-Saharan Africa. An environment that does not support growth in labor demand tends not to support high returns to basic education. This conclusion is supported by detailed econometric studies of the relationship between education and earnings in Ghana, where private returns to primary school in the late 1980s were estimated at only a few percentage points.[10] The lack of attractive economic returns to attending school also helps explain the disturbing trend in many Sub-Saharan African countries of declining primary school enrollment since 1980.[11] Households' perception that the benefits of education no longer justify its costs has been a factor in this decline.

Thus the low educational attainment of Sub-Saharan Africa's labor force perpetuates low rates of growth that in turn discourage households from educating their children—a "vicious circle." Experience elsewhere argues that the vicious circle can be broken. Many countries in Southeast Asia lacked an educated work force but were nevertheless able to grow rapidly and simultaneously to expand education. Less than twenty years ago workers in Indonesia and Thailand averaged about four years of schooling, but since these economies have taken off, primary enrollment has become virtually universal and gross secondary enrollment rates have risen to more than 30 percent. The capabilities of their workers did not prevent these countries from initiating economic growth, and Sub-Saharan Africa's situation should be no different.

A similar argument can be made concerning training. The lack of industrialization in Sub-Saharan Africa probably has little to do with the lack of trained workers. In a better climate for industry training will take place, as it does elsewhere, mostly within enterprises and on the job. Evidence suggests that on-the-

Box 3. Zambia and Chile: A tale of two copper countries

At independence in 1964 Zambia's per capita income was higher than that in all Sub-Saharan African economies except South Africa. The government set out to improve living standards, raise education levels, and distribute the fruits of the country's natural resources. The boom in copper prices in the late 1960s added to the government's capacity to fund social projects, and Zambia's efforts in human and physical capital accumulation were enormous. Primary, secondary, and technical enrollments increased by 44, 75, and 46 percent. Investment was an extraordinary 48 percent of GDP between 1965 and 1974, falling to a (still remarkable) 30 percent for the entire period of 1969–91. Yet economic growth averaged just 1.1 percent a year from 1965 to 1991, well below the 3 percent annual rate of population growth. What went wrong?

The crash of copper prices in the mid-1970s probably influenced the timing of Zambia's economic collapse, but the seeds of the crisis were planted by economic policy choices. An overvalued exchange rate, high tariffs on finished products, and low tariffs on intermediate and capital goods discouraged both the use of local resources and the expansion of nontraditional exports. These distorted incentives led to investment in capital-intensive production, despite the relative abundance of labor, and employment in the formal sector stagnated.

In industrial policy the government focused on establishing parastatals. The hope was that parastatals would provide training, create jobs, encourage rural development through backward linkages, overcome the extreme risk aversion of domestic entrepreneurs, and promote social objectives by selling goods at low prices. Faced with this array of objectives, many incompatible with efficient enterprise management, the industrial sector failed to deliver on most, and many enterprises became a drain on public finances.

Agricultural policy also was aimed at circumventing the market. The goal was to control the cost of food while ensuring its availability to the general population. When these two conflicting objectives created a gap between the incentive prices for farmers and the low prices for consumers, the difference was made up from the government budget. Fertilizer subsidies were intended to benefit poor farmers, but wealthy commercial farmers ended up receiving more than 90 percent of the subsidy. Zambia's agricultural policies accelerated the destruction of traditional agriculture, pushing rural workers into urban areas.

The combined effect of industrial and agricultural support ultimately drained the public sector budget and has contributed to price inflation of 100 percent a year since 1988. By 1990 real income per capita in Zambia was almost 40 percent below 1965 levels.

Chile's story is different. In the 1970s, after four decades of experimenting with wealth redistribution policies, Chile introduced radical changes in its economic policy approach. The new approach focused on enhancing the role of the private sector in a market-based development strategy. Policymakers' first priority was to control inflation by reducing the large public sector deficit. The first stage of policy reforms also included freeing retail prices, liberalizing domestic capital markets, privatizing some state-owned enterprises, and reducing import barriers.

The second phase consisted of seven reforms to redefine the role of the state and its interaction with the private sector in order to enhance market efficiency. The "seven modernizations" comprised reforms of the labor law, social security, the education system, health services, land and water rights, the judicial system, and administrative practices (including decentralization of government functions). The result was a modern regulatory framework that set rules guaranteeing free entry and property rights. Appropriate regulations increased competitive pressures, expanded the range of possible transactions, and encouraged investment.

How did these changes affect workers? The experience of Atacama, a region in northern Chile, is illustrative. In 1970 Atacama was far from a center of opportunity for workers. The desert region offered a handful of jobs in the modern copper mining sector and attracted tourists to observe traditional gold and silver mining. The population was concentrated in two cities, Copiapo and Vallenar, that had developed a reasonable commercial and service economy but that had had little growth for many decades. In the mid-1970s the landscape of the region began to change. Between 1973 and 1986 the area planted with vineyards expanded by more than seventy times, growth made possible by computerized drip irrigation. Growth in the fruit-packing industry soon followed, creating significant seasonal employment. By the late 1980s laborers' wages in Atacama's agricultural area of Copiapo were the highest in Chile, and thousands of people traveled from other regions for the harvest season. In mining foreign investors brought in new technology and built infrastructure. And as new investment revitalized the coast, the fish unloaded increased from 1,100 tons in 1973 to 236,000 tons in 1986. With the growth in economic activity, commercial establishments more than quadrupled, and the number of hotels and tourist facilities increased fifteenfold.

The economic base of the Atacama region did not change because of a discovery: the desert, the sea, the minerals, and the irrigation technology could have been combined in production before. Instead, policy changes induced the transformation in investors' behavior: better incentives to produce for the export market, and legal reforms that clearly delimited public and private sector responsibilities, reducing the uncertainty associated with economic policy.

job training is already widespread in Sub-Saharan Africa's informal sector, where apprenticeships are common.

The stock of human capital in Sub-Saharan Africa is not the explanation for the region's poor growth performance. But that does not mean that governments can be complacent about investing in human capital. Growth and the reduction of poverty require a human resource strategy that enhances worker capabilities, a strategy that is consistent with growth-oriented macroeconomic and sector policies. If households perceive an increase in remunerative opportunities, they will invest in human capital. But governments must still play a role, identifying appropriate areas of intervention and efficiently allocating their own resources to improve the health, nutrition, education, and training of their citizens.

Although other World Bank reports identify specific human resource development strategies, some general principles can be stated here.[12] First, where private returns are high but investments are not being undertaken, governments must understand why so that they can design appropriate interventions, especially pricing strategies. Free primary education may be warranted to capture positive externalities and to achieve distributional objectives. But for other human resource programs free provision is less likely to be necessary, and alternatives should be pursued.[13]

Second, where government intervention is warranted, it need not take the form of public production and delivery. Governments should focus more on financing, encouraging fair competition between public and private suppliers, and removing restrictions on private suppliers of health, education, or training services.

Third, in directing public resources toward human capital, governments should avoid benefiting the privileged few—as much of the spending on university education in Sub-Saharan Africa does—and instead expand the human capital base of the economy. The highest priority should be investing in children, because their health, nutrition, and basic education provide the human capital foundation of a nation's future.

•   •   •

Labor outcomes generally have not improved in Sub-Saharan Africa over the past three decades, either in absolute terms or relative to those in other developing regions. The disappointing trends appear to have been due more to problems of labor demand than to problems of labor supply, the result of a lack of opportunities for African workers and not a shortage of workers or skills.

CHAPTER 4

Marginalization in the World Economy

By almost any measure the global economy is becoming more integrated. International trade as a share of world output has roughly doubled in the past two decades. Financial flows across borders are on the rise. Private capital directed to developing economies, whether foreign direct investment or financial assets, has reached record levels. International migration between the North and South may show less sign of growth, but remittances from migrants to their countries of origin have become a leading source of foreign exchange for many economies.

These trends are generally associated with improving labor outcomes, especially in low- and middle-income economies. Growth in exports as a share of GDP is associated with more rapid increases in real wages and the expansion of employment opportunities. Capital flows have supplemented domestic savings, and when these resources have contributed to productive investments, labor has benefited. Through both permanent and temporary migration labor, like capital, has sought its highest return, increasing individual earnings and improving household welfare, often through remittances.

But not all workers or regions have benefited. Trade creates jobs, but it also leads to the loss of jobs in import-competing industries; foreign capital that was not productively invested has contributed to macroeconomic crises, with labor bearing the subsequent costs of adjustment; and migration has broken families apart and produced political and social backlashes in host countries. Although these are real costs that need to be recognized and, where appropriate, addressed by policies, the net effects for workers of international engagement remain positive.

Sub-Saharan Africa and the global economy

Sub-Saharan Africa, however, has not been part of this process. Rather than becoming more integrated into global markets, the region has been marginalized.[14] It is important to understand what this means (Table 3). Sub-Saharan Africa's marginalization is apparent not in the level of its dependence on trade but in how slowly its exports are growing.

In 1993 Sub-Saharan Africa's exports amounted to less than 2 percent of world exports—certainly a small share. But South Asia's share is even smaller (less than one percent), and Latin America's, though twice as large (3.6 percent), is still marginal. Relative to its share of world GDP, Sub-Saharan Africa's share of world exports is actually larger than that of any other region except East Asia.[15] And at 27 percent, Sub-Saharan Africa's share of exports in GDP is comparable to the 30 percent share in the successful economies of East Asia and twice the shares in Latin America and South Asia.

But between 1965–80 and 1980–93 both Sub-Saharan Africa and the Middle East and North Africa have witnessed a sharp fall in export growth, while Latin America, East Asia, and South Asia have all had increased growth. And net foreign direct investment remains low in Sub-Saharan Africa. Meanwhile the region leads all others in receipts of official development assistance. Finally, Sub-Saharan Africa's share of global migration also is small, with migrants from the region accounting for a negligible amount of the migration from South to North (Box 4).

Although the benefits of participation in global markets are apparent for some regions, most obviously East Asia, some have argued that participation has hurt rather than helped Sub-Saharan Africa. The region's comparative advantage remains in primary products, for which the terms of trade continue to decline. As a result Sub-Saharan Africa has received fewer and fewer of the gains from trade. And capital flows to the region in the 1970s contributed to its debt problem today, with debt service part of the drain on Africa's resources.

But neither of these arguments is a persuasive case for Sub-Saharan Africa's disengaging from international economic relations. Other regions have faced adverse terms-of-trade movements, but have adjusted and prospered (Figure 6). Confronted with similar commodity price shocks, the countries of Southeast Asia expanded their links to world markets—by diversifying their exports (including the types of primary products), investing in agriculture to improve productivity, and pursuing more prudent macroeconomic strategies in response to changing international conditions. Southeast Asia found ways to escape the trap of declining terms of trade that continues to plague Sub-Saharan Africa. Similarly, Sub-Saharan Africa's debt burden today represents missed opportunity: the debt problem is primarily the result not of taking advantage of foreign capital,

The marginalization of Sub-Saharan Africa is evident in the slow growth of its exports

Table 3. Regional participation in international trade and capital flows
(percent)

Region	Share of world GDP 1993	Share of world exports 1993	Share of exports in GDP 1993	Average annual growth of exports 1965–80	Average annual growth of exports 1980–93	Primary product exports as a share of total exports 1992	Share of net foreign direct investment[a] 1992	Official development assistance as share of GNP 1993
World	100.0	100.0	21	6.5	5.0	25	—	—
Sub-Saharan Africa	1.2	1.7	27	6.1	2.5	76	2.8	11.5
East Asia and the Pacific	5.6	8.3	30	8.5	10.8	26	47.5	0.8
South Asia	1.4	0.9	13	1.8	7.3	27	1.3	1.5
Middle East and North Africa	2.1	2.8	32	5.7	–1.0	90	2.8	3.2
Latin America and the Caribbean	6.1	3.6	14	–1.0	3.4	62	33.5	0.3
High-income economies	79.0	78.3	20	7.3	5.1	18	—	—

— Not applicable.
Note: All regional averages are dollar-based totals for the regions, except for the share of primary product exports, for which country shares are averaged-using total country exports as weights.
a. As a share of total for low- and middle-income economies.
Source: World Bank 1992, 1994b, and 1995c.

Box 4. Transnational migration inside Africa

South-North migration from Sub-Saharan Africa is relatively small. But within the region cross-border migration is a major social and economic phenomenon. Nomadic groups in the Sahel historically have moved great distances in search of grazing lands or to sell stock. Extended families and ethnic groups, split by what from a historical perspective seem arbitrary national boundaries, often cross porous borders. Economic cycles of boom and bust have encouraged migration, with millions joining the Nigerian labor force when oil prices were high and large numbers settling in Côte d'Ivoire during that nation's period of prosperity. Wars have added tens of millions of refugees fleeing one nation for another. A pervasive lack of information makes estimating the size of these movements difficult. But one attempt, based on available labor force and population surveys, suggests that Africa, with only 10 percent of the world's population, may have half the world's nationals abroad (Stalker 1994).

South Africa, a major destination for Sub-Saharan migrants for the past century, is once again attracting large numbers. People from throughout the region are migrating to South Africa in response to economic opportunities and the political opening of the country. But these movements pose dilemmas for South Africans, just as migration does in the United States, European countries, the Gulf states, and other countries. Migrants can be viewed as an additional resource that will help to raise South Africa's income, as the traditional movement of workers from countries bordering South Africa to the Witwatersrand mines has been. But migration is not without costs, especially because migrants are likely to compete with domestic unskilled labor. With unemployed and discouraged workers close to 40 percent of the labor force in South Africa, uncontrolled migration could worsen an already explosive domestic labor market situation. Managing migration may be necessary to avoid the intergroup conflicts now occurring in some European countries.

Managing migration may be an appropriate policy response for South Africa, but lessons from elsewhere suggest that restricting migration is not easy. The greater the incentives to migrate, the more difficult and expensive it becomes to ration entry and the more likely that illegal migration will occur. Selling the right to citizenship, establishing temporary work arrangements, and restricting the access of migrants to social services and the other entitlements of citizens are instruments for managing migration that have been used in other regions.

Other regions have also faced adverse movements in terms of trade

Figure 6. Terms of trade for selected country groups, 1970–92

(1970=100)

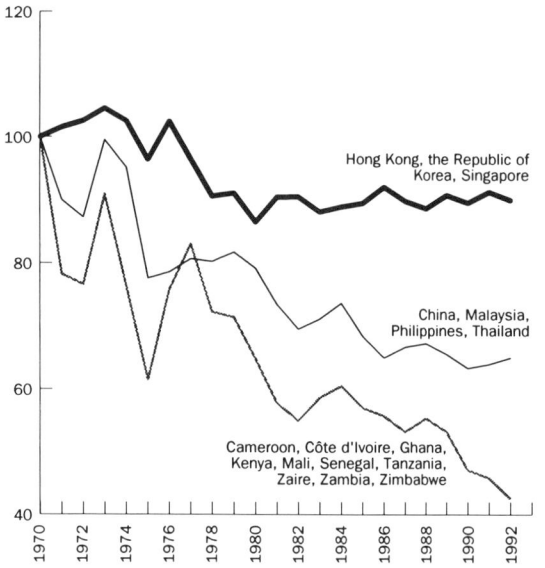

Note: Terms of trade are the average price of a country's exports relative to the average price of its imports. The indexes are unweighted means for each country group.
Source: World Bank data; Lewis and McPherson 1994.

but of misusing foreign capital—through capital flight and poorly conceived investments.

Sub-Saharan Africa's retreat from world markets must be reversed. Labor depends on an increase in the derived demand for its services, and single economies provide markets that are too limited. The benefits of trade for labor have been realized by the successful economies of East Asia, and they are recognized today even by the world's largest low-income economies, China and India. Trade also allows workers to shop for consumption goods where they are the cheapest and permits firms to acquire the equipment and technologies that best complement the skills of

their workers. Recent world economic history suggests that Sub-Saharan Africa's workers will be better served by an increase in international trade and that capital flows to finance productive investment can support more rapid economic growth.

Increasing Sub-Saharan Africa's participation in the world economy

Development strategies based on overvalued exchange rates and import controls until recently dominated Africa's economic landscape. But since the late 1980s many economies have initiated the macroeconomic reforms necessary to increase international trade and encourage inflows of foreign capital. In a range of countries black market premiums have been dramatically reduced, and in the Communauté financière africaine (CFA) franc zone the January 1994 devaluation of the CFA franc was a step toward renewed external competitiveness. Equally encouraging are improvements throughout the region in agricultural pricing policies, reduced reliance on direct price and import controls, and liberalization of credit allocation and interest rates. Yet there is still far to go on the macroeconomic agenda. Some countries have not reversed their long-standing inward orientation, and more must be done across the region in such areas as trade and fiscal reform.[16]

But macroeconomic policy has not been the only reason for Africa's marginalization in the global economy. In countries that have proceeded with macroeconomic reform neither exports nor foreign investment have taken off. The greater riskiness of most African economies and deficiencies in the institutional preconditions for investment are additional constraints. In the face of frequent policy turnarounds investors, both domestic and foreign, remain wary of government commitment to reforms. The lack of well-established property rights and of mechanisms of dispute resolution further discourages investors. And the absence of complementary inputs—especially basic infrastructure—lowers the productivity of both labor and capital.[17]

•   •   •

Continuing with macroeconomic reform, rehabilitating infrastructure, reducing risk, and proceeding with institutional reforms are all part of the agenda for encouraging economic transactions between Sub-Saharan Africa and the rest of the world. African workers stand to gain from such initiatives.

CHAPTER 5

A Long Agenda of Labor Reforms

Governments have an important role to play in improving labor outcomes. A market-based development strategy requires an environment that encourages productive investments by households, farms, and firms. A stable macroeconomy is vital to this process, as are the protection of property rights and the provision of public goods. Governments need to correct market failures, such as constraints on borrowing for human capital investments that may limit the education, health, and nutrition of children. Governments also must pursue policies (maintaining a stable real exchange rate) and support institutions (a well-functioning customs authority) that permit an economy to reap the benefits of participation in the international economy. The experience of different regions suggests that government actions in these areas can have a profound effect on the economic well-being of workers. But should governments also intervene directly in labor markets to influence labor outcomes?

Worldwide, governments do intervene—by setting labor standards (minimum wages, occupational health and safety), legislating income and job security (pensions, rules governing dismissals), and influencing industrial relations (workers' rights to organize, industrial courts). The motivation for doing so is clear. Governments often consider labor market outcomes to be harsh, unfair, or otherwise undesirable, and they employ labor policies in an attempt to circumvent or override market-determined outcomes. Examples from Sub-Saharan Africa include high minimum wages in the early 1980s in Zimbabwe, tripartite agreements for setting wages and expanding employment in Kenyan enterprises, generous maternity benefits in Cameroon, and restrictions on hiring and firing in Senegal.

Regardless of the intention of such direct interventions in labor markets, the legacy of many has not been positive—and Sub-Saharan Africa's experience is no exception. Regulations aimed at improving wages or working conditions can discourage investment or, for a given level of investment, discourage the use of labor. And by improving the circumstances of a relatively few "insiders" fortunate enough to have secured jobs protected by labor standards, the government creates a constituency dependent on the system of protection and economic rents that finance their privileged position.

The structure of Sub-Saharan Africa's economies, heavily dependent on smallholder agriculture, means that the overwhelming majority of workers lie beyond the reach of most labor standards and legislation. Most African workers neither are hired through nor compete in labor markets as these are conventionally understood. Instead, a worker's earnings and work conditions are determined mostly by product market outcomes and his or her entrepreneurial and technical skills and access to capital, land, infrastructure, and technology. The plight of rural women merits special emphasis—their arduous work days contain many tasks, each carried out at low productivity with techniques that have changed little over time. Directives issued in national capitals on minimum wages or maternity benefits are likely to have little impact on this huge segment of Sub-Saharan Africa's labor force.

For those workers beyond the reach of direct government interventions in the labor market, economic welfare will be determined primarily by the overall package of reforms required to restore growth to the region. Labor policies alone cannot overcome the negative effects of an otherwise distorted economic environment. But they are important as complements to other reforms.

Improving labor outcomes through labor policy

The most important principle that should guide labor policies in Sub-Saharan Africa is that interventions should be attuned to market realities. If they are not, they are likely to discourage investment, to promote rent-seeking, or to be ignored. None of these outcomes is in labor's interest. The following paragraphs discuss different types of interventions.

Child labor

The vast majority of working children in Sub-Saharan Africa are unpaid helpers on family farms. Most people do not condemn this work by children as long as they continue to attend school. Children working as prostitutes, soldiers, and in factories are most often the subject of domestic and international concern and outrage. In Sub-Saharan Africa, where the manufacturing sector is small and heavily protected, and thus the incentives to employ children are limited, there is less child labor in factories than in other regions.

In Sub-Saharan Africa the problem of child labor is reflected primarily in its mirror image—low and often declining rates of school attendance even at the primary level. Changing the incentives households face can encourage school attendance, and thus discourage child labor. For example, antipoverty programs decrease a family's reliance on child income. And lowering the direct costs of schooling or providing financial incentives to attend school can increase attendance. After the elimination of school fees and mandatory uniforms in Malawi, primary school enrollments increased substantially.[18]

Legislation, including a ban on child labor, may be the least effective approach. Analysis of legislative bans suggests that they are likely to be effective only where there is a capable administration determined to implement the laws, it is difficult for employers to conceal the use of child labor, and, most important, there is little economic advantage to employers or families from children working.[19] In low-income settings these conditions are unlikely to hold. But banning child labor may still be an important part of a strategy to increase public awareness and involvement. It may also be an effective tool when narrowly focused on the most egregious forms of exploitation of a nation's young workers.

Health and safety standards

Most Sub-Saharan African workers operate in rural and informal markets where legislated labor standards are ineffective in dealing with health and safety concerns. For agricultural and informal workers health and safety conditions can be improved through general policies aimed at the environment in which they work. The use of dangerous chemicals in agriculture, for example, is usually best controlled by regulation of the import or production of pesticides and fertilizers. Similarly, efforts to provide safe drinking water in rural areas and improve sanitary conditions in villages and urban slums can have a profound impact on the welfare of the working-age population.

The Onchocerciasis (Riverblindness) Control Program in West Africa is one of the world's most successful programs for improving the health of rural workers. Onchocerciasis, a disease that eventually causes blindness, has long been referred to as a "plague upon the land" because of its devastating impact on rural workers' health and well-being. The Onchocerciasis Control Program was started in 1974 by seven African countries—later expanded to eleven—with support from more than twenty bilateral and multilateral donors. The program has eliminated parasites in the human population in more than 60 percent of the eleven-country area and protects more than 30 million people against contracting the disease. It is estimated that by 1995 the program had prevented more than 250,000 cases of blindness, freed 25 million hectares of land from the disease and thus opened it to resettlement and cultivation, and

made an additional one million person-years of productive labor available.[20]

In Sub-Saharan Africa health and safety interventions in the formal sector will reach fewer workers than interventions in rural areas. But nearly all countries legislate minimum health and safety standards aimed at protecting formal sector workers. These standards usually are justified on the grounds that employers are aware of workplace dangers but workers may not be. Even if workers are aware of occupational risks, they may accept dangerous jobs because they have little alternative. Poor countries will be unable to enforce the same level of labor standards as richer economies, so they usually need to focus their limited administrative capacity where it will do the most good.

One difficulty in setting standards is determining their level or stringency. Reducing hazards in the workplace is costly. Typically, the greater the reduction in hazards, the more it costs. These costs may fall on employees through lower wages or reduced employment. So setting standards too high can lower the welfare of workers, but setting them too low may fail to adequately deal with the risks workers face. The appropriate level is one at which the costs are commensurate with the value that informed workers place on improved working conditions and reduced risk. There is no magic formula. In many countries this level is determined through consultations among the government, employers, and workers. Trade unions and other civic organizations can play a role in helping to set and then enforce these standards.

Minimum wages

Proponents argue that minimum wages can raise the incomes of poorly paid workers at little or no cost to overall employment and thus are an effective means of redistributing income. Opponents counter that minimum wages increase production costs and reduce employment, resulting in higher wages for "insiders" and lower wages for the working poor, who must now compete against an even larger pool of labor in the informal or unregulated sector of the economy. Which effect minimum wages have depends on many factors, including the competitiveness of product markets, the level at which the minimum wage is set, and the government's ability to enforce it. Evidence from Sub-Saharan Africa suggests that minimum wages have done little to improve the situation of most workers.[21]

Minimum wages have a long history in Africa. They were set relatively high in Tanzania's estate sector in the late 1960s and in Zimbabwe in the early 1980s, but in both cases proved unsustainable. Macroeconomic decline in Sub-Saharan Africa during the 1980s caused most minimum wages to decline precipitously in real terms as governments raised them by less than inflation. In Mauritius high minimum wages for male workers in export processing zones before 1984 were associated with slower growth in male employment. The government eliminated minimum wages for men after noticing that the zones' demand for female workers, covered by a lower minimum, exceeded supply while male unemployment remained high. After the minimum was eliminated male recruitment rose sharply, and in January 1995 wages paid to men settled at less than the old minimum wage.[22]

Income and job security

Sharp drops in income from work can have a profound impact on the living standards of workers and their families. Unemployment, disability, and old age are important causes of poverty in all countries, and of deeper poverty for those who are already poor. Most societies have developed ways of coping with income insecurity and the threat to living standards from both expected and unexpected falls in income. Often these strategies involve some combination of private saving, informal support mechanisms, and obligations on employers. But households may find it difficult to borrow to cover temporary falls in labor income. Community support mechanisms may break down in an economywide shock, and they tend to decline with urbanization and the diminishing importance of the extended family. And private insurance markets for unemployment, disability, and old age may be limited or absent. Government involvement is needed when these private or informal solutions prove insufficient.

Public works programs can be an important government response to income insecurity, especially in rural areas. These programs, designed to help the unemployed poor, use low wages as a self-targeting mechanism to ensure that only the truly needy will accept the job. Wages that are too high may attract better-off workers and, given limited budgets, lead to fewer jobs for the truly destitute. These schemes are particularly appropriate during economic downturns when other job opportunities are unavailable. They are also well suited for rural areas during the slack season, and can have a secondary benefit of building or maintaining important infrastructure assets. In Ethiopia program participants have been employed in building roads and preventing soil erosion; in Zimbabwe the Food for Work Program provides employment and a basic level of consumption for some of the poor.[23]

Income security is also an issue for workers in the modern sector. One approach is regulations that make it difficult for private firms or public employers to lay off workers. Job security legislation is needed to limit unfair practices and protect workers against arbitrary dismissals. But some countries have designed legislation to protect workers against job loss for many reasons. Even when economic circumstances—whether firm-specific or economywide—call for employment cuts, job security legislation can impede necessary adjustments.

Used in this manner, job security legislation can hinder job creation. In essence, prohibitions on firing become prohibitions on hiring. Employers affected by overly restrictive job security regulations become reluctant to take on the long-term obligation of hiring an employee and may instead rely on casual labor or subcontracting or simply choose not to expand even when circumstances are favorable. The net result may be job protection for the few at the cost of slower overall job creation. These effects of job security provisions have been identified in Senegal and Zimbabwe and are likely occurring elsewhere in the region.[24]

When governments get involved in providing income security to formal workers through job security provisions, social assistance, and pensions, getting the design of these interventions right is important. Beneficiaries, usually better-off workers, often gain at the expense of other workers (in the case of job security regulations) or of future generations (in the case of pensions).

Pay and employment in the public sector

In Sub-Saharan Africa there are thousands of public employees—teachers and police officers, agricultural extension workers and accountants, cabinet ministers and clerks—who are dedicated to their work and provide essential services. But in many countries public employment has done little to enhance growth. Too often public employment is associated with inadequate provision of public goods and services by the civil service, inefficient production by state enterprises, fiscal deficits and macroeconomic instability, and distortion of the labor market.[25]

Transforming the public sector—from one that is a drag on economic growth to one that promotes it—requires institutional, political, and economic interventions. Pay and employment reform may include retrenchment and salary decompression (widening the pay differential between skilled and unskilled workers), privatization of state enterprises, demobilization of armies, decentralization of social services, and elimination of job guarantees to school graduates. But certain basic principles are common to all elements of the reform package. They include reconciling public employment levels with public output targets and designing incentives to motivate public workers. The principle that labor policies should be attuned to market realities is especially applicable to the management of Sub-Saharan Africa's public sector work force.

Throughout Sub-Saharan Africa the low productivity of the public sector has more often been the result of inadequate incentives than of incapable workers. This does not imply that qualified people are in abundant supply, but greater productivity is possible with the available skills. Often public workers who are absent, lackadaisical, or unproductive in government posts are actively pursuing secondary employment as entrepreneurs, traders, or farmers. Elsewhere, loss-making state enterprises have become profitable not by replacing their work forces but by creating environments that reward the performance of existing workers.

Pay and employment practices in the civil service and state enterprises in Sub-Saharan Africa have deviated from what the market would prescribe. All too common are excessive public hiring (especially of the unskilled), precipitous erosion in compensation, severe salary compression, and an inflated aggregate wage bill. The consequences for public sector performance have been disastrous: low morale, high absenteeism and moonlighting, difficulties in attracting and retaining professionals, a breakdown in supervision and discipline, and a lack of complementary inputs needed to carry out tasks (Box 5).

Recognition of the systemic decline of the state sector has prompted governments to undertake public sector pay and employment reform programs. Ghana pursued an ambitious civil service reform program, decompressing salary differentials (measured as the ratio of the top of the government pay scale to the bottom) from a low of 2.5:1 in 1984 to 10:1 in 1991. To help finance this move toward more adequate pay levels for senior staff, and to create a government work force consistent with government resources, nearly 60,000 Ghanaian civil servants, roughly 20 percent, were retrenched. These reforms initially brought modest decreases in the ratio of the government wage bill to GDP, intended to free resources for nonlabor inputs, but a large pre-election wage increase in 1992 reversed this progress.

The good news from Ghana and elsewhere is that it is possible to implement many of the instruments of civil service pay and employment reform. Technical, legal, and political obstacles proved surmountable. The bad news is that the ultimate objectives—restoring fiscal balances and improving the performance of the government sector—remain elusive.

Box 5. Low public sector pay leads to poor public sector performance

A recent study of the failures of public road maintenance in Africa draws attention to the deterioration in public sector pay for engineers as a binding constraint on improved performance. It concludes that human resource constraints are the single most important issue facing most road agencies. These agencies suffer from an acute shortage of technically qualified staff and employ redundant, unskilled workers. Salaries in some road agencies are so low that daylighting, the practice of performing another full-time job during regular working hours, has become common.

The shortage of technical staff and the practices of daylighting and moonlighting are attributed to the growing gap between civil service salaries and the pay for comparable positions in the private sector (Box Table 2). An engineer working in the private sector generally earns more than twice as much as his public sector counterpart (in Tanzania and Zambia, five and nine times as much). And real salaries have declined sharply. A young engineer in Tanzania who would have earned about $250 a month in 1970 now earns a real salary of only $20 a month. Similarly, in Nigeria until about five years ago, a young engineer earned about $1,000 a month, but could now expect to earn only $150 a month.

Roads departments that pay qualified technical staff a fraction of the going market wage end up with high vacancy rates (as in Kenya, Malawi, Mozambique, Uganda, and Zambia), with expatriate road managers paid through donor-financed technical assistance programs (as in Botswana, Lesotho, Namibia, Rwanda, Tanzania, and Zambia), or with staff forced to supplement their incomes by moonlighting, daylighting, manipulating allowances, and pilfering. The net result is a road agency that cannot be managed effectively.

Source: Adapted from Heggie 1995.

Engineers earn far more in the private sector

Box Table 2. Incomes of public and private sector engineers in selected countries, 1993
(dollars per month)

	Cameroon	Kenya	Nigeria	Rwanda	Tanzania	Uganda	Zambia	Zimbabwe
Public salary	377	170	154	186	70	99	70	370
Private salary	777	465	334	661	350	360	600	600
Private/public	2.1	2.7	2.2	3.6	5.0	3.6	8.6	1.6

Note: Comparisons are of salaries and allowances for graduate engineers with three to four years of practical experience. Conversion to dollars at January 1994 exchange rates, after CFA franc devaluation.
Source: Heggie 1995.

Retrenching government workers and reforming pay levels and structures are not enough. Institutional reforms to restore accountability are essential, including staff recruitment and promotion policies that are tied to individual performance and not to inflexible rules or patronage. Sub-Saharan African governments must also rethink the scope of government activity. In too many countries the public sector is overextended, with too many agencies, departments, and enterprises charged with too broad a range of responsibilities. Governments need to rely more on private sector delivery and to expose more elements of the public sector to market forces.

Unions

Wherever people work together in large numbers they tend to form organizations, often trade unions, to defend their rights and advance their interests. Whether these organizations have positive or negative effects on economic growth and on the conditions of most workers is controversial. Opponents of unions view them as monopolists that limit employment to raise their members' wages and, through these higher wages, reduce business profits, discourage investment, and slow aggregate growth. Trade unions also are seen as obstructionists that wield political power against economic reforms that might jeopardize their privileged "insider" positions. The net result is fewer jobs and lower wages for "outsiders," the vast majority of workers who do not participate in the unionized sectors of the economy.

Union supporters see things differently. Unions give workers a collective voice and enhance productivity and wage equality. At the plant level unions improve the balance of power between labor and management and limit employer behavior that is arbitrary, exploitative, or retaliatory. By establishing grievance procedures, unions reduce turnover and promote job stability and thus enhance worker productivity. Union activities can also establish labor standards that spill over into the rest of the economy and benefit all workers. And at the national level unions have supported democratic movements in countries as diverse as the Republic of Korea, Poland, South Africa, and the United States.

Which of these two faces of trade unionism prevails depends on many factors, including the relative size of the wage sector, the economic environment in which trade unions operate, government interventions in industrial relations, and the behavior of unions themselves.

Given the dominance of smallholder agriculture in Sub-Saharan African economies, the percentage of the labor force that is unionized remains quite low and the nature of industrial relations has little impact on the circumstances of the overwhelming majority of workers. In the wage sector the role of unions generally is also limited. Many Sub-Saharan African governments have effectively prohibited independent trade unions, and unions in the wage sector, heavily dominated by public employment, are mostly public sector unions closely allied with the government.

That is not to say that Sub-Saharan Africa lacks a history of independent trade unionism. The trade union movement in Kenya, for example, played an important role in the national struggle for independence. More recently, COSATU (Congress of South African Trade Unions), CSC (Confederation Syndicale du Congo), NLC (National Labor Congress) in Nigeria, and ZCTU (Zambia Congress of Trade Unions) have been at the forefront of pro-democracy movements in their respective countries.[26] Some of these same union movements have also played a significant role in the economic sphere, bargaining for better wages and working conditions for their members. The significance of the natural resource sector in the economy often was a factor in a union's power.

In analyzing the role of trade unions in Sub-Saharan Africa there is merit in distinguishing between economies in which unions represent a large number of workers and those in which the number of unionized workers is small. The effects of unions certainly vary with the unions' size. But the basic principles that should guide government policy toward labor organizations do not. The policy goal should always be to create an environment that minimizes the negative monopoly tendencies of unions and instead encourages their productivity- and welfare- enhancing features.

Three policy rules are consistent with this objective. First, product markets need to be competitive. When product markets are uncompetitive because of trade protection or government subsidies, unions have greater opportunity to act as monopolists and to extract some of the prevailing economic rents. They will be encouraged to ally themselves politically with their employers and with politicians who perpetuate their protected positions. But under competitive conditions responsible union leaders will be reluctant to jeopardize the employment of union members and will be cautious about raising wages above the level dictated by increases in labor productivity.

Second, governments must protect the right of workers to organize and impose penalties on employers who violate this principle. Competition between trade unions for members also should be permitted. Not only are such provisions consistent with the basic human right of freedom of association, but competition between unions and a framework for contestable union elections limit the potential monopoly power of any single labor organization.

Third, the parties engaged in bargaining must be made to internalize the costs of outcomes rather than shift them to third parties. This principle has many applications. If labor law stipulates that workers should be paid even when on strike, labor's incentive to reach a settlement is compromised. If labor and management in parastatals know that the government will cover enterprise deficits, taxpayers, not enterprise managers and workers, will end up bearing the cost of the settlement. Similarly, industrywide agreements—common in Zambia—can be a barrier to entry, especially for small firms, and can lead to wage settlements that are passed on to consumers in the form of higher prices. More decentralized bargaining permits product market competition to act as a constraint on wage settlements, encouraging unions and employers to agree to pay increases that are in line with improvements in productivity. In general, the body of labor regulations—the coverage of collective agreements, the system of industrial courts, sanctions against "sympathy" or general strikes—should be designed both to internalize costs and to ensure due process for both workers and employers.

With few exceptions, trade unions are not major economic actors in Sub-Saharan Africa. But that does not mean that governments should ignore industrial relations. Good industrial relations serve two important functions in Sub-Saharan Africa. First, they help attract investment. And second, they make it less likely that governments will intervene directly in setting wages and establishing working conditions and thus that public officials will usurp the role of markets in allocating resources, a practice at the root of much of Sub-Saharan African's economic woes.

•   •   •

Improving labor outcomes in Sub-Saharan Africa is crucial to reducing poverty and enhancing the welfare of millions of African households. The agenda of needed reforms is long, and countries must establish priorities. A set of basic principles can guide the direction of policy. These principles include relying more on markets than on governments to allocate resources, making sure that interventions are attuned to labor market realities, and minimizing the use of policies that favor a small group of "insiders" over the masses of poor "outsiders." Beyond these general principles, specific labor reforms require an evaluation of their costs and benefits, including their efficiency implications and distributional and political consequences.

CHAPTER 6

Adjustment's Effects on Workers

Over the past decade Sub-Saharan Africa has struggled to restart economic growth. After years of continued macroeconomic decline many countries have embarked on ambitious reform agendas. Some, like Ghana, have pushed through reform programs that are starting to bear modest fruit. But other countries—such as Nigeria, Somalia, and Zaire—remain stuck in old development strategies or mired in civil unrest. These countries have experienced negative growth rates and continuing deterioration in the living standards of their workers.

Are reforms good for workers?

Many of the reforms that are key to economic transformation are good for workers and especially for the poor, even in the short run. Trade liberalization and depreciation of the exchange rate together promote exports, which tend to be intensive in low-skilled labor. The removal of pervasive biases against agriculture also helps the poor, who are disproportionately concentrated in rural areas. The development of the private sector often means the growth of new businesses in labor-intensive sectors. And because tradables account for a smaller part of the consumption basket of poor people than of that of the well-off, the poor are less affected by rising relative prices of imports.

In Sub-Saharan Africa poor rural workers have mostly gained from adjustment. Although affected by macroeconomic decline, rural workers have benefited from the removal of the pro-urban biases that pervaded the old, import-substituting regimes. Where price changes have improved the terms of trade for agriculture, rural workers have gained even before the overall economy started to grow. Real agricultural wages in Ghana rose by 27 percent following adjustment. But unskilled urban workers and many of those employed in the public sector have lost from the reforms.

Governments can help speed the transition and ease the plight of displaced workers through policies aimed at making labor markets more adaptable (Box 6). For example, they can incorporate into their adjustment strategies reforms to promote labor mobility (such as the reform of labor codes in Senegal) and transfer programs to reduce the burden on those who lose their jobs (such as Ghana's severance pay for displaced public sector workers).

Box 6. Labor market information

Improving the information available to participants in labor markets is important to the performance of these markets and to their contribution to economic growth and poverty reduction. Employers need information on wages, and on the number and qualifications of workers available at those wages, to make staffing and training decisions. Job seekers need information on wages and on jobs available at those wages to guide their education, training, and career choices. And policymakers must combine all this information to monitor an economy's performance and develop effective labor market policies.

Much of this information is generated through informal networks of market participants. Information on a job opening at a nearby factory may be passed along to a job seeker by friends and relatives, and the wages offered by competitors may be learned by quizzing job applicants. But these informal information sources are rarely sufficient for ensuring that labor markets clear or for setting policy. There is therefore a need for the public sector to play a role in the delivery of labor market information, especially in Sub-Saharan Africa, where such efforts have been minimal.

Experience in other regions yields several lessons that can guide the cost-effective design of labor market statistical and information systems: (1) identify a base statistics program from which to build; (2) link statistics to user needs; (3) use collection techniques that build on the strengths of different data sources; (4) connect collection with analysis of statistics; (5) devote resources to timely processing, analysis, and dissemination; (6) weigh the advantages of a central statistical agency; (7) protect the integrity and objectivity of statistics; (8) invest in professional staff; and (9) acknowledge the long-term commitment required.

Source: Adapted from Goldfarb and Adams 1993.

Can the informal sector be an engine of growth in Sub-Saharan Africa?

The informal sector, however defined, accounts for a significant share of employment in much of Sub-Saharan Africa. Many see the informal sector as a dynamic feature in an otherwise stagnant economic landscape. It is easy to see why. The formal sector, dominated by government, state enterprises, and protected private interests, has failed to grow and increasingly is a drain on the rest of the economy. Foreign investment has retreated from the region, and agriculture, long discriminated against, has shown limited signs of recovery. By comparison, some see the informal sector as well-endowed with entrepreneurial talent and vibrant with economic activity.

Can policymakers tap into this potential? And if so, can the informal sector play a vital role in the region's revival? To help it do so, policies that constrain the informal sector should be removed as part of a more market-based development strategy. Price controls and government monopolies limit the profitability of commercial activities and reduce employment in trading activities. Restrictions on interest rates constrain the growth of informal establishments by limiting their access to credit. Government procurement policies often implicitly favor large contracts and thereby discriminate against small enterprises.

Policy reforms in these areas will allow the growth of more firms and the transformation of informal into formal activities.

But efforts to reform policies that distort markets in ways that discriminate against informal establishments should not turn into policy efforts to discriminate in favor of such establishments. Providing heavily subsidized credit to small establishments is itself a form of policy distortion, and there is little evidence to suggest that such interventions lead to a net gain for economies or employment. Because of the high cost of administering small loans, and the high failure rate of informal enterprises, subsidized credit programs directed at small ventures often yield a low economic return.

The informal sector does have a vital role to play in Sub-Saharan Africa's economic future. But so do Africa's formal sector and its vast agricultural sector. Labor-demanding growth does not call for keeping wages below their market level or interest rates above theirs. Labor-demanding growth calls for removing barriers that artificially protect some segments of the economy while constraining others (Box 7). In other regions informal sector establishments have played an important role in generating productive employment when market access has been relatively unconstrained and where they have complemented, not substituted for, formal establishments.

Box 7. A proactive policy agenda for the informal sector

A market-based strategy toward the informal sector does not mean laissez-faire. The institutional environment required to support the development and growth of small and medium-size enterprises requires re-regulation, not just deregulation. Two examples follow of how governments can improve the functioning and efficiency of markets in which informal sector firms find themselves at a disadvantage.

Government procurement. Rules and practices governing public procurement often are biased in favor of large-scale enterprises, many of which are capital-intensive or foreign-owned or both. These biases include the size of public projects, the legal and technical requirements of bidding procedures, and long delays between bids and contractor selection and between services rendered and payment. To overcome these barriers, many governments have reformed their procurement policies, especially for public works (including construction of rural roads, construction of schools, and road rehabilitation and maintenance). One of the most successful programs is Senegal's AGETIP (*Agence d'exécution des travaux d'intérêt public contre le sous-emploi*, or Agency for the Execution of Public Works against Underemployment). Since 1989 this agency has delivered

cost-efficient public works and created tens of thousands of temporary job opportunities. Among the policy reforms key to AGETIP's success have been the breakdown of large public works projects into modules appropriate for small contractors, the simplification of legal and technical documents, and timely payments by government agencies to contractors (Pean and Watson 1993).

Microfinance. Small enterprises often are constrained by a lack of credit. General macroeconomic reforms and liberalization of the financial sector are likely to improve credit opportunities for all firms, including those in the informal sector. But governments can go further by providing incentives to encourage the growth of financial intermediaries serving small enterprises in both urban and rural areas. To overcome the shortage of financial intermediaries, one approach is to establish a second-tier or "apex" institution that provides institutional development grants or capitalization to lenders who meet transparent performance criteria. The level of access to funds can be made to depend on loan and cost recovery rates. Training in financial skills and in retailing financial services at the local level may also be called for. These approaches are being used in Ethiopia and South Africa.

CHAPTER 7

Risk—and Opportunity

W hat are the prospects for workers in Sub-Saharan Africa as they approach the next century? Some recent events bode well for the future. Since the late 1980s many countries in the region have made progress in macroeconomic reforms. The overvalued exchange rates and resulting black market premiums that have long characterized the region have been reduced dramatically, in some countries to near zero. There have been major improvements in agricultural pricing policy and reduced reliance on direct price and import controls. These reforms reflect what might be a "silent revolution" in economic thinking among the region's policymakers. Accompanying these changes in economic orientation are moves toward political liberalization—including dozens of contestable elections—which would have been considered unlikely only six or seven years ago.[27]

But any optimism about Africa's prospects must be tempered by the region's historical record. The optimism about economic prospects during the era of independence turned out to be unwarranted. The initial success of the Kenyan and Ivoirian economies proved unsustainable. Civil wars and genocidal campaigns continue to plague the region and, when they occur, erase any hope of proceeding with the development agenda. And the specter of AIDS, with its impact on the labor force, its claim on public expenditures, and its human toll, remains an ominous threat to the region (Box 8).

Improvements in labor market outcomes for Sub-Saharan African workers will depend on the selection of good domestic and international policies. To illustrate this point, *World Development Report 1995* developed a model of the world economy that simulates regional outcomes using different assumptions about policy directions. Two cases are presented. The "low case" is based largely on the persistence of past trends: investment rates do not rise, school enrollment rates do not change, and labor productivity continues to grow slowly. Internationally, trade

---

Box 8. AIDS in Sub-Saharan Africa

The AIDS epidemic in Sub-Saharan Africa will have far-reaching effects on workers and their families. An estimated 3.4 million urban and 1.9 million to 4.3 million rural African adults are infected with HIV, the virus that causes AIDS. The prevalence of HIV among low-risk adults in some rural areas is estimated to be over 16 percent in Zambia, over 10 percent in Tanzania, and under 4 percent in Cameroon and Côte d'Ivoire. In urban areas prevalence rates reach as high as 30 percent in Uganda and over 20 percent in Botswana. In the region as a whole 2.5 to 3.6 percent of the adult population may be HIV-positive. Predicting how the infection will spread and what its consequences will be is difficult not only because of a lack of data on infection rates but because of an inability to judge behavioral responses to the epidemic.

Unlike other, more prevalent diseases in Sub-Saharan Africa, AIDS strikes primarily adults in their most productive years, leading to a large direct loss in households' labor income. But there are additional effects on household economic welfare. As individuals infected with HIV become sick with AIDS, household time (primarily that of women and children) is allocated away from production to caring for the sick. Children may be taken out of school to care for family members, reducing the amount of education they receive. In rural areas the loss of household labor time can lead to a reduction

in the variety of crops produced and a switch from cash to subsistence crops. The cumulative effect is to decrease both a household's current income and its ability to deal with shocks, reducing food security and increasing the risk of poverty.

AIDS strikes members of all socioeconomic groups, but in urban areas HIV prevalence increases with educational attainment. The resulting loss of skilled labor is a huge liability for firms and slows aggregate growth. Observers in several countries have speculated that absenteeism and fatigue on the job due to AIDS may be more costly, in terms of lost output, than deaths due to AIDS. Because much of the financing for the treatment of AIDS patients comes from savings—which leads to lower capital accumulation—the impact on workers is perpetuated.

Predicting the impact of AIDS on economic growth is difficult not only because of the uncertainty surrounding the spread of the disease, but also because the epidemic affects both output growth and demographics. Studies predict a sustained fall in the growth rate of GDP per capita of 0.3 to 0.5 percentage point a year, depending on the assumptions used. This is a significant decline in what is already a low-growth environment.

Source: Adapted from Ainsworth and Over 1994.

Policies consistent with the "high case" will lead to large wage increases for African workers

Table 4. Sub-Saharan Africa's economic performance under two scenarios, 1994–2010
(percent, except where otherwise specified)

	Low-case scenario	High-case scenario
Factor accumulation		
Investment as a share of GDP (period average)	16.0	25.0
Educational attainment of labor force (average years of schooling by 2010)	2.7	3.0
Total factor productivity (annual growth rate)	0.5	1.5
Output growth		
GDP per capita (annual growth rate)	–0.3	1.7
Exports (annual growth rate)	3.6	6.6
Wage growth		
Unskilled labor (total growth)	0.4	50.7
Skilled labor (total growth)	9.5	49.3

Source: World Bank 1995c.

protection remains at current levels. The "high case" assumes the opposite. Strong domestic policy action is combined with rising international integration, leading to increasing investment rates, declining school dropout rates, technology transfer, rising international capital flows, and liberalization of international trade.

These simulations suggest that Sub-Saharan Africa's workers can expect significant increases in their real wages if policies consistent with the "high case" are adopted (Table 4). If investment rates are raised to 25 percent of GDP, the educational attainment of the work force rises, and resources are allocated more efficiently, growth in regional GDP per capita will turn positive, and export growth will double. These trends will result in real wages in 2010 that are 50 percent higher than those today. But if the economic policies of today persist, most African workers will experience little change in their already difficult situations.

The results of the simulation model are not intended as forecasts of the near future, but they are indicative of the consequences for workers of the policy directions that governments choose. There is a risk that the world economy will move on, leaving much of Africa behind. But there is also an opportunity for Sub-Saharan Africa to follow other regions toward growth in job creation, productivity, and real wages for its expanding labor force.

Notes and References

Notes

1. Poverty is defined here as surviving on less than $1 per person per day. Estimates of the extent of absolute poverty in Sub-Saharan Africa refer to 1992 and are from World Bank (1994a).

2. Estimates of the distribution of the working-age population by economic activity are based on estimates and projections from the ILO (1986), ILO updates, and country sources. Because of the paucity of data in Sub-Saharan Africa, these estimates may be subject to a high degree of error. For the region as a whole estimates are based on findings for fifteen to twenty countries representing 30 to 55 percent of the region's working-age population. The estimate of the size of the region's informal sector, as a weighted average, is strongly influenced by an estimate of 37 percent for employment in Nigeria's informal sector. Specific data and methodology are reported in Filmer (1995).

3. Women are 80 percent of those recorded as out of the labor force in East Asia and the Pacific, 64 percent in Europe and Central Asia, 80 percent in Latin America and the Caribbean, 84 percent in the Middle East and North Africa, 75 percent in OECD countries, 86 percent in South Asia, and 80 percent in Sub-Saharan Africa. All figures are based on ILO (1986).

4. For 1985/86 Newman (1988) reports unemployment rates in Côte d'Ivoire of 20.0 percent for Abidjan, 2.9 percent for other urban areas, 0.1 percent for rural areas, and 2.9 percent for the nation as a whole. Double-digit urban unemployment rates in the 1980s are also reported by AERC (1991) and Turnham (1993) for Botswana, Ethiopia, Kenya, Lesotho, Nigeria, Senegal, Zambia, and Zimbabwe. The World Bank (1995a) indicates that unemployment rates in Cameroon's capital, Yaounde, rose from 7 percent to 25 percent between 1983 and 1993.

5. Estimates are from Nehru and Dhareshwar (1991) and Nehru, Swanson, and Dubey (1993). They compute capital stocks, both physical and human, using a perpetual inventory model. These stocks are augmented according to investment rates for physical capital and enrollment rates for human capital, and depreciate with time and mortality.

6. The conclusions of the simple bivariate analysis whose results are presented in Figure 5 are supported by more rigorous econometric analysis, including that by Barro (1991), Levine and Renelt (1992), and Easterly and Levine (1994).

7. Although the focus here is on education rather than health or nutrition, similar arguments would hold for those forms of human capital.

8. These data are from the World Bank (1991 and 1995c) and refer to a weighted average for the region, with weights reflecting population shares.

9. Nehru, Swanson, and Dubey (1993) report mean years of schooling in Sub-Saharan Africa for those aged fifteen to sixty-four of 0.8 year in 1960 and 2.6 years in 1987. Ahuja and Filmer (1995) report an estimated increase from 3.0 to 4.0 years in 1985–95 for the population aged six to sixty, excluding those currently attending school.

10. This result is from Glewwe (1991). Bennell (1994) reaches a similar conclusion, disputing the more traditional position (as in Psacharopoulos 1988) that primary education yields high returns in all low-income countries, including those in Africa.

11. These trends are discussed in World Bank (1995b).

12. See, for example, World Bank (1986 and 1991, ch. 3).

13. For example, although increased consumption of micronutrients such as iodine and vitamin A can yield a high economic return by increasing both mental and physical capabilities at low cost, that does not mean that nutritional supplements should be distributed free of charge. A better use of scarce public resources might be nutrition education. Similarly, if tertiary education yields a high economic return, student loans, not free tuition, may be sufficient to induce the desired investment.

14. This is the theme of the treatment of Sub-Saharan Africa in ILO (1995), which draws from Collier (1994).

15. The ratio of regional share of world exports to share of world GDP is 1.5 for East Asia, 1.4 for Sub-Saharan Africa, 1.3 for the Middle East and North Africa, 1.0 for high-income economies, and 0.6 for South Asia and Latin America.

16. Recent macroeconomic reforms in Sub-Saharan Africa are discussed in Bouton, Jones, and Kiguel (1994) and World Bank (1995b).

17. For a more complete analysis, see Collier (1994).

18. School uniforms had cost $3.00, ten times the school fees. A publicity campaign to encourage children to attend school and the public's response to increased democraticization also contributed to the increase in enrollments (*The Economist*, February 1995).

19. For a review of legislation prohibiting child labor, see Grootaert and Kanbur (1994).

20. The Onchocerciasis Control Program and its effects are discussed in Cooley and Benton (1995).

21. This holds whether there is a national or sectoral minimum wage (Zimbabwe's pre-1990 industrial minimum) or a

structure of minimum wages (Senegal's *salaire grille*) by occupation and experience. The more disaggregated approach of a minimum wage structure can, in theory, be tuned to market circumstances, but in practice it is more likely to exacerbate distortions in the wage structure.

22. Minimum wages in Tanzania, Zimbabwe, and Mauritius are analyzed in Sabot (1988), Fallon (1987), and Robinson (1994). Trends in real minimum wages in Sub-Saharan Africa are presented in Freeman (1992).

23. See von Braun (1994) for more discussion of public works programs in Sub-Saharan Africa and elsewhere.

24. Job security provisions in Senegal are evaluated by Terrell and Svejnar (1989) and in Zimbabwe by Fallon and Lucas (1991).

25. Pay and employment policies in the government sector are extensively discussed in Lindauer and Nunberg (1994). Analyses of these issues in state enterprises can be found in Banerji and Sabot (forthcoming) and Lindauer (1991).

26. A survey of the role of trade unions in recent democratic movements in Africa appears in ICFTU (1991).

27. See World Bank (1995b) for discussion of trends in Sub-Saharan Africa over the half decade 1988–93.

References

AERC (African Economic Research Consortium). 1991. *Employment Issues in Sub-Saharan Africa.* AERC Special Papers Series 14. Nairobi.

Ahuja, Vinod, and Deon Filmer. 1995. "Educational Attainment in Developing Countries: New Estimates and Projections Disaggregated by Gender." Background paper to *World Development Report 1995.* World Bank, Washington, D.C.

Ainsworth, Martha, and Mead Over. 1994. "AIDS in African Development." *World Bank Research Observer* 9 (2): 203–40.

Banerji, Arup, and Richard H. Sabot. Forthcoming. "Barriers to Labor Reform in Developing Country Public Enterprises." *World Development.*

Barro, Robert J. 1991. "Economic Growth in a Cross-Section of Countries." *Quarterly Journal of Economics* 106 (2): 407–43.

Bennell, Paul. 1994. "Rates of Return to Education: Does the Conventional Pattern Prevail in Sub-Saharan Africa?" Institute of Development Studies Working Paper 10. Institute of Development Studies, Brighton, United Kingdom.

Bouton, Lawrence, Christine Jones, and Miguel Kiguel. 1994. "Macroeconomic Reform and Growth in Africa: Adjustment in Africa Revisited." Policy Research Working Paper 1394. World Bank, Washington, D.C.

Collier, Paul. 1994. "The Marginalisation of Africa." Centre for the Study of African Economies, Oxford, United Kingdom.

Cooley, Laura, and Bruce Benton. 1995. "Controlling Riverblindness in West Africa." In World Bank, *Investing in People: The World Bank in Action.* Washington, D.C.

Easterly, William, and Ross Levine. 1994. "Africa's Growth Tragedy." World Bank, Policy Research Department, Macroeconomics and Growth Division, Washington, D.C.

The Economist. "A Lesson from Malawi." February 25, 1995, page 43.

Fallon, Peter R. 1987. "The Labor Market in Zimbabwe: Historical Trends and an Evaluation of Recent Policy." Development Research Department Discussion Paper 296. World Bank, Washington, D.C.

Fallon, Peter R., and Robert E. B. Lucas. 1991. "The Impact of Changes in Job Security Regulations in India and Zimbabwe." *World Bank Economic Review* 5 (3): 395–413.

Filmer, Deon. 1995. "Estimating the World at Work." Background paper to *World Development Report 1995.* World Bank, Washington, D.C.

Freeman, Richard B. 1992. "Labor Market Institutions and Policies: Help or Hindrance to Economic Development?" In *Proceedings of the World Bank Annual Conference on Development Economics 1991.* Washington, D.C.: World Bank.

Glewwe, Paul. 1991. *Schooling, Skills, and the Returns to Government Investment in Education: An Exploration Using Data from Ghana.* Living Standards Measurement Study Working Paper 76. Washington, D.C.: World Bank.

Goldfarb, Robert S., and Arvil V. Adams. 1993. *Designing a System of Labor Market Statistics and Information.* World Bank Discussion Paper 205. Washington, D.C.

Grootaert, Christiaan, and Ravi Kanbur. 1994. "Child Labor: A Review." Policy Research Working Paper 1454. World Bank, Washington, D.C.

Heggie, Ian. 1995. *Management and Financing of Roads: An Agenda for Reform.* World Bank Technical Paper 275, Africa Technical Series. Washington, D.C.

ICFTU (International Confederation of Free Trade Unions). 1991. "Joint BFTU (Botswana Federation of Trade Unions)/ICFTU Panafrican Conference on Democracy, Development and the Defence of Human and Trade Union Rights." Paper presented at the conference, July 9–11, Gaborone, Botswana.

ILO (International Labour Organization). 1986. *Economically Active Population Estimates and Projections: 1950–2025.* Geneva: International Labour Office.

_____. 1995. *World Employment 1995.* Geneva: International Labour Office.

_____. Various years. *Yearbook of Labor Statistics.* Geneva: International Labour Office.

Levine, Ross, and David Renelt. 1992. "A Sensitivity Analysis of Cross-Country Growth Regressions." *American Economic Review* (September): 942–63.

Lewis, Jeffrey D., and Malcolm F. McPherson. 1994. "Macroeconomic Management: To Finance or Adjust?" In

David L. Lindauer and Michael Roemer, editors, *Asia and Africa: Legacies and Opportunities in Development*. San Francisco: Institute for Contemporary Studies Press.

Lindauer, David L. 1991. "Parastatal Pay Policy in Africa." *World Development* 19(7): 831–38.

Lindauer, David L., and Barbara Nunberg, editors. 1994. *Rehabilitating Government: Pay and Employment Reform in Africa*. Washington, D.C.: World Bank.

Mazumdar, Dipak. 1994a. "The Structure of Wages in African Manufacturing." World Bank, Africa Regional Office, Office of the Chief Economist, Washington, D.C.

———. 1994b. "Wages in Africa." World Bank, Africa Regional Office, Office of the Chief Economist, Washington, D.C.

Nehru, Vikram, and Ashok Dhareshwar. 1991. "A New Database on Physical Capital Stock: Sources, Methodology and Results." *Revista de Analisis Economico* 8(1):37–59.

Nehru, Vikram, Eric Swanson, and Ashutosh Dubey. 1993. "A New Database on Human Capital Stock: Sources, Methodology and Results." Policy Research Working Paper 1124. World Bank, Washington, D.C.

Newman, John L. 1988. *Labor Market Activity in Côte d'Ivoire and Peru*. Living Standards Measurement Study Working Paper 36. Washington, D.C.: World Bank.

Pean, Leslie, and Peter Watson. 1993. "Promotion of Small-Scale Enterprises in Senegal's Building and Construction Sector: The 'AGETIP' Experience." In Organization for Economic Cooperation and Development (OECD), *New Directions in Donor Assistance to Micoenterprises*. Paris.

Psacharopoulos, George. 1988. "Education and Development: A Review." *World Bank Research Observer* 3 (1): 99–116. Washington, D.C.

Robinson, Derek. 1994. "Do Standards for the Workplace Help or Hurt?" Background paper for *World Development Report 1995*. World Bank, Washington, D.C.

Sabot, Richard. 1988. "Tanzania." In Stephen Herzenberg and Jorge F. Perez-Lopez, editors, *Labor Standards and Development in the Global Economy*. U.S. Department of Labor, Washington, D.C.

South African Bureau of Statistics. 1968. *South African Statistics*. Pretoria.

Stalker, Peter. 1994. *The Work of Strangers: A Survey of International Labour Migration*. Geneva: International Labour Office.

Tanzania Bureau of Statistics. 1971. *1967 Population Census*, vol. 4, *Economic Statistics*. Dar es Salaam.

———. 1992. *1988 Population Census, National Profile, Basic Demographic and Socio-Economic Characteristics*. Dar es Salaam.

Terrell, Katherine, and Jan Svejnar. 1989. *The Industrial Labor Market and Economic Performance in Senegal: A Study in Enterprise Ownership, Export Orientation, and Government Regulation*. Boulder, Colo.: Westview Press.

Turnham, David. 1993. *Employment and Development: A Review of Evidence*. Paris: OECD.

UNIDO (United Nations Industrial Development Organization). Various years. *Industrial Statistics Yearbook*. New York.

Union Bank of Switzerland. 1994. *Prices and Earnings around the Globe*. Zurich.

von Braun, Joachim. 1994. "Employment for Poverty Reduction and Food Security." Paper presented at an International Policy Workshop sponsored by International Food Policy Research Institute, October, Airlie House, Virginia.

World Bank. 1986. *Financing Education in Developing Countries: An Exploration of Policy Options*. Washington, D.C.

———. 1991. *World Development Report 1991: The Challenge of Development*. New York: Oxford University Press.

———. 1992. *World Development Report 1992: Development and the Environment*. New York: Oxford University Press.

———. 1994a. "The Many Faces of Poverty: Status Report on Poverty in Sub-Saharan Africa." Africa Technical Department, Human Resources and Poverty Division. Washington, D.C.

———. 1994b. *World Development Report 1994: Infrastructure for Development*. New York: Oxford University Press.

———. 1995a. "Cameroon: Diversity, Growth, and Poverty Reduction." Report 13167CM. Central and Indian Ocean Department, Population and Human Resources Division. Washington, D.C.

———. 1995b. "A Continent in Transition: Sub-Saharan Africa in the Mid-1990s." Africa Regional Office. Washington, D.C.

———. 1995c. *World Development Report 1995: Workers in an Integrating World*. New York: Oxford University Press.

World Development Report 1995

Workers in an Integrating World

Full text edition available in the following languages:

English (Hardback)	ISBN 0-19-521103-0	Stock No. 61103	$37.95
English (Paperback)	ISBN 0-19-521102-2	Stock No. 61102	$19.95

Forthcoming:

Arabic	ISBN 0-8213-2897-2	Stock No. 12897	$19.95
Chinese	ISBN 0-8213-2896-4	Stock No. 12896	$19.95
French	ISBN 0-8213-2892-1	Stock No. 12892	$19.95
German	ISBN 0-8213-2894-8	Stock No. 12894	$19.95
Japanese	ISBN 0-8213-2895-6	Stock No. 12895	$19.95
Portuguese	ISBN 0-8213-2899-9	Stock No. 12899	$19.95
Russian	ISBN 0-8213-2898-0	Stock No. 12898	$19.95
Spanish	ISBN 0-8213-2893-X	Stock No. 12893	$19.95

Regional Perspectives on World Development Report 1995

Seven companions to *World Development Report 1995*, each with additional material on the labor market issues in the particular region.

Labor and the Growth Crisis in Sub-Saharan Africa
ISBN 0-8213-3343-7   Stock No. 13343 $6.95
Jobs, Poverty, and Working Conditions in South Asia
ISBN 0-8213-3344-5   Stock No. 13344 $6.95
Involving Workers in East Asian Growth
ISBN 0-8213-3345-3   Stock No. 13345 $6.95
Will Arab Workers Prosper or Be Left Out in the Twenty-First Century?
ISBN 0-8213-3346-1   Stock No. 13346 $6.95
Workers in Transition in Europe and Central Asia
ISBN 0-8213-3347-X   Stock No. 13347 $6.95
Labor and Economic Reform in Latin America and the Caribbean
ISBN 0-8213-3348-8   Stock No. 13348 $6.95
The Employment Crisis in Industrial Countries: Is International Integration to Blame?
ISBN 0-8213-3349-6   Stock No. 13349 $6.95

For order coupon, see back of this booklet

World Development Report on CD-ROM 1978-95

A complete archive of all 18 World Development Reports.

Now, for the first time, a new CD-ROM product, created by ASIA-CD, Hong Kong, a copublisher of the World Bank, brings you all 18 editions of the Report together with the World Development Indicators 1995. With its easy-to-use but powerful search engine, this product gives you an invaluable resource and a comprehensive database on the development debate. Specifications: Windows 3.1; Minimum 4MB free RAM 386 or faster processor; CD-ROM drive to MPC Level 1 specification.

Forthcoming
Stock No. 31590 / Single-user version: $375.00 / Multi-user version $750.00

Available in the U.S. from the World Bank and Oxford University Press. For availability in other countries, contact:

Asia 2000 Ltd.
Attn: Edowan Bersma, Sales & Circulation Dept
46-48 Wyndham Street
Winning Centre, 7th Floor
Central, Hong Kong

World Development Indicators 1995
World Bank Data on Diskette

Statistical tables providing instant access to the most comprehensive and current data available on social and economic development in more than 200 economies. Topics range from agricultural production to international trade. Included in the print version of the Report, the Indicators are also available separately on diskette. Each package includes a user's guide to the ☆STARS☆ retrieval system and a 3½" double-density diskette for PCs with a hard disk, at least 512K RAM, and MS-DOS version 2.1 or higher.

ISBN 0-8213-2921-9 / Stock No. 12921 / $45.00

For order form, see back of this booklet

Distributors of World Bank Publications

ARGENTINA
Carlos Hirsch, SRL
Galeria Guemes
Florida 165, 4th Floor-Ofc. 453/465
1333 Buenos Aires

Oficina del Libro Internacional
Alberti 40
1082 Buenos Aires

AUSTRALIA, PAPUA NEW GUINEA, FIJI, SOLOMON ISLANDS, VANUATU, AND WESTERN SAMOA
D.A. Information Services
648 Whitehorse Road
Mitcham 3132
Victoria

AUSTRIA
Gerold and Co.
Graben 31
A-1011 Wien

BANGLADESH
Micro Industries Development
  Assistance Society (MIDAS)
House 5, Road 16
Dhanmondi R/Area
Dhaka 1209

BELGIUM
Jean De Lannoy
Av. du Roi 202
1060 Brussels

BRAZIL
Publicacoes Tecnicas Internacionais
  Ltda.
Rua Peixoto Gomide, 209
01409 Sao Paulo, SP

CANADA
Le Diffuseur
151A Boul. de Mortagne
Boucherville, Québec
J4B 5E6

Renouf Publishing Co.
1294 Algoma Road
Ottawa, Ontario K1B 3W8

CHINA
China Financial & Economic
  Publishing House
8, Da Fo Si Dong Jie
Beijing

COLOMBIA
Infoenlace Ltda.
Apartado Aereo 34270
Bogota D.E.

**COSTA RICA, BELIZE, GUATE
-MALA, HONDURAS,
NICARAGUA, PANAMA**
Chispas Bookstore
75 Meters al Norte del Hotel Balmoral
  en calle 7
San Jose

COTE D'IVOIRE
Centre d'Edition et de Diffusion
  Africaines (CEDA)
04 B.P. 541
Abidjan 04 Plateau

CYPRUS
Center of Applied Research
Cyprus College
6, Diogenes Street, Engomi
P.O. Box 2006
Nicosia

CZECH REPUBLIC
National Information Center
P.O. Box 668
CS-113 57 Prague 1

DENMARK
SamfundsLitteratur
Rosenoerns Allé 11
DK-1970 Frederiksberg C

EGYPT, ARAB REPUBLIC OF
Al Ahram
Al Galaa Street
Cairo

The Middle East Observer
41, Sherif Street
Cairo

FINLAND
Akateeminen Kirjakauppa
P.O. Box 23
FIN-00371 Helsinki

FRANCE
World Bank Publications
66, avenue d'Iéna
75116 Paris

GERMANY
UNO-Verlag
Poppelsdorfer Allee 55
53115 Bonn

GREECE
Papasotiriou S.A.
35, Stournara Str.
106 82 Athens

HONG KONG, MACAO
Asia 2000 Ltd.
46-48 Wyndham Street
Winning Centre
7th Floor
Central, Hong Kong

HUNGARY
Foundation for Market Economy
Dombovari Ut 17-19
H-1117 Budapest

INDIA
Allied Publishers Private Ltd.
751 Mount Road
Madras - 600 002

INDONESIA
Pt. Indira Limited
Jalan Borobudur 20
P.O. Box 181
Jakarta 10320

IRAN
Kowkab Publishers
P.O. Box 19575-511
Tehran

IRELAND
Government Supplies Agency
4-5 Harcourt Road
Dublin 2

ISRAEL
Yozmot Literature Ltd.
P.O. Box 56055
Tel Aviv 61560

R.O.Y. International
P.O. Box 13056
Tel Aviv 61130

Palestinian Authority/Middle East
Index Information Services
P.O.B. 19502 Jerusalem

ITALY
Licosa Commissionaria Sansoni SPA
Via Duca Di Calabria, 1/1
Casella Postale 552
50125 Firenze

JAMAICA
Ian Randle Publishers Ltd.
206 Old Hope Road
Kingston 6

JAPAN
Eastern Book Service
Hongo 3-Chome, Bunkyo-ku 113
Tokyo

KENYA
Africa Book Service (E.A.) Ltd.
Quaran House, Mfangano St.
P.O. Box 45245
Nairobi

KOREA, REPUBLIC OF
Daejon Trading Co. Ltd.
P.O. Box 34
Yeoeida
Seoul

MALAYSIA
University of Malaya Cooperative
  Bookshop, Limited
P.O. Box 1127, Jalan Pantai Baru
59700 Kuala Lumpur

MEXICO
INFOTEC
Apartado Postal 22-860
14060 Tlalpan, Mexico D.F.

NETHERLANDS
De Lindeboom/InOr-Publikaties
P.O. Box 202
7480 AE Haaksbergen

NEW ZEALAND
EBSCO NZ Ltd.
Private Mail Bag 99914
New Market
Auckland

NIGERIA
University Press Limited
Three Crowns Building Jericho
Private Mail Bag 5095
Ibadan

NORWAY
Narvesen Information Center
Book Department
P.O. Box 6125 Etterstad
N-0602 Oslo 6

PAKISTAN
Mirza Book Agency
65, Shahrah-e-Quaid-e-Azam
P.O. Box No. 729
Lahore 54000

Oxford University Press
5 Bangalore Town
Sharae Faisal
P.O. Box 13033
Karachi-75350

PERU
Editorial Desarrollo SA
Apartado 3824
Lima 1

PHILIPPINES
International Book Center
Suite 720, Cityland 10
Condominium Tower 2
Ayala Avenue, H.V. dela
  Costa Extension
Makati, Metro Manila

POLAND
International Publishing Service
Ul. Piekna 31/37
00-577 Warszawa

PORTUGAL
Livraria Portugal
Rua Do Carmo 70-74
1200 Lisbon

SAUDI ARABIA, QATAR
Jarir Book Store
P.O. Box 3196
Riyadh 11471

SINGAPORE, TAIWAN
Gower Asia Pacific Pte Ltd.
Golden Wheel Building
41, Kallang Pudding, #04-03
Singapore 1334

SLOVAK REPUBLIC
Slovart G.T.G. Ltd.
Krupinska 4
P.O. Box 152
852 99 Bratislava 5

SOUTH AFRICA, BOTSWANA
Oxford University Press
  Southern Africa
P.O. Box 1141
Cape Town 8000

SPAIN
Mundi-Prensa Libros, S.A.
Castello 37
28001 Madrid

Librería Internacional AEDOS
Consell de Cent, 391
08009 Barcelona

SRI LANKA & THE MALDIVES
Lake House Bookshop
P.O. Box 244
100, Sir Chittampalam A.
  Gardiner Mawatha
Colombo 2

SWEDEN
Fritzes Customer Service
Regeringsgatan 12
S-106 47 Stockholm

Wennergren-Williams AB
P.O. Box 1305
S-171 25 Solna

SWITZERLAND
Librairie Payot
Case postale 3212
CH 1002 Lausanne

Van Diermen Editions Techniques
P.O. Box 465
CH 1211 Geneva 19

TANZANIA
Oxford University Press
Maktaba Street
P.O. Box 5299
Dar es-Salaam

THAILAND
Central Books Distribution Co. Ltd.
306 Silom Road
Bangkok

TRINIDAD & TOBAGO, JAMAICA
Systematics Studies Unit
#9 Watts Street
Curepe
Trinidad, West Indies

UGANDA
Gustro Ltd.
1st Floor, Room 4, Geogiadis Chambers
P.O. Box 9997
Plot (69) Kampala Road
Kampala

UNITED KINGDOM
Microinfo Ltd.
P.O. Box 3
Alton, Hampshire GU34 2PG
England

ZAMBIA
University Bookshop
Great East Road Campus
P.O. Box 32379
Lusaka

ZIMBABWE
Longman Zimbabwe (Pte.) Ltd.
Tourle Road, Ardbennie
P.O. Box ST 125

Order Form

CUSTOMERS IN THE UNITED STATES:
Complete this coupon and return to
**The World Bank
Box 7247-8619
Philadelphia, PA 19170-8619
U.S.A.**
To have your order shipped faster, charge
by credit card by calling (202) 473-1155
or send this completed order coupon by facsimile
by dialing (202) 676-0581.

CUSTOMERS OUTSIDE THE UNITED STATES:
Contact your local World Bank publications
distributor for information on prices in local currency
and payment terms. If no distributor is listed for your
country, use this order form and return it to the U.S.
address. **Orders that are sent to the U.S. address
from countries with distributors will be returned to
the customer.**

Quantity	Title	Stock No.	Price	Total

* SHIPPING AND HANDLING charges are $5.00 per
order. If a purchase order is used, actual shipping will be
charged. For air mail delivery outside the United States,
add $8.00 for one item plus $6.00 for each additional
item.

Subtotal US$ _____

Shipping and Handling* US$ _____

Total US$ _____

CHECK METHOD OF PAYMENT

❑ Enclosed is my check payable to The World Bank.

❑ Charge my ❑ VISA ❑ MasterCard ❑ American Express

_____
Credit card account number

_____
Expiration date   Signature

❑ Bill me. (Institutional customers only. Purchase order must be included.)

PLEASE PRINT CLEARLY

Name _____

Address _____

_____

City _____ State _____ Postal Code _____

Country _____ Telephone _____

1163